Eugene B

Mc...

[reviewed 6/3 for the
American Hist Rev]

SOCIAL REFORMERS IN URBAN CHINA
The Chinese Y.M.C.A., 1895–1926

Harvard East Asian Series 56

The East Asian Research Center at Harvard University
administers research projects designed to further
scholarly understanding of China, Japan, Korea, Vietnam,
and adjacent areas.

Social Reformers in Urban China

THE CHINESE Y.M.C.A., 1895–1926

Shirley S. Garrett

HARVARD UNIVERSITY PRESS, CAMBRIDGE
MASSACHUSETTS, 1970

Distributed in Great Britain by Oxford University Press, London
Printed in the United States of America
Preparation of this volume has been aided by a grant from the Ford
Foundation
Library of Congress Catalog Card Number 74–133218
SBN 674–81220–4

To Jim, Joe, and Gussie

ACKNOWLEDGMENTS

Of the many people whose good will and help made this book possible, I should like to single out a few. My lifelong friend, Mrs Irene Myers Daitch, gave me the courage to leave another career behind and enter on the long road of Chinese studies. I owe an immeasurable personal and intellectual debt to my teacher and friend, John K. Fairbank. Mrs. Virginia Downes and Miss Shirley Leslie of the Y.M.C.A. Historical Library have been unfailingly helpful. Finally, my husband has served as unofficial editor of the manuscript and has shown gallantry beyond the call of duty. To all of these lovely people, I offer my thanks.

CONTENTS

SOCIAL REFORMERS IN URBAN CHINA
The Chinese Y.M.C.A., 1895–1926

1

THE SEARCH FOR COMMUNICATION

By the early years of the twentieth century, a few social reformers already viewed Chinese cities with a mixture of hope and dismay. In centers such as Shanghai and Tientsin there existed the wealth and energy to create a revitalized nation. At the same time, swiftly growing and modernizing urban areas were themselves creating new social problems. Some reformers therefore saw the need not only to develop the creative energies of the city, but also to keep urban society from destroying itself: in short, to make and keep the Chinese city a place fit to live in.

Of the many private groups concerned with facets of this huge problem, a number were Western in inspiration or origin. Some were as ephemeral as a puff of dust. Others, however, left a distinct imprint on their environment. To examine their histories is to realize that the two cultures could exchange ideas, and that both Westerner and Chinese could on occasion demonstrate considerable flexibility. A study of Western reform movements in urban China is particularly rewarding in that it not only affords a view of Chinese cities during this confused century, but also illuminates the possibilities and pitfalls of Sino-Western cultural diffusion.

During the first quarter of the twentieth century, probably the most widely recognized organ of private social planning in China was an institution both Chinese and Western in nature, a transplant from the United States that successfully took root in China. This organization was the Chung-kuo Chi-tu Chiao Ch'ing-nien hui or Chinese Y.M.C.A., formally founded on December 8, 1895. Although its roots lay in evangelical Christianity and its early financial support was meager, the Association

2

soon built a self-supporting and secular constituency among urban Chinese of the student and business classes. Within fifteen years it was a powerful organizing force among young Chinese on the mainland and in Tokyo, and began to play a constructive role in the long epic of Chinese reform. Thereafter its works and the techniques of organization developed by it helped recognizably to shape the destinies of modern China. Founder of the first youth association in the country, pioneer in education, health, and welfare programs, developer if not originator of communitywide urban action, the Association was for a time able to harness diverse energies in the changing country to meet the demands of modern urban life.

A study of the Chinese Y.M.C.A. involves many countries and traditions, for the Association's roots lie deep and broad —in the famine areas of Shansi, the mills of Liverpool, the seminaries of America, the court intrigues of Peking. The Y.M.C.A. entered China at a promising time for a Western institution. Since the middle of the nineteenth century, war, famine, and foreign intrusion had gnawed at China's vitals, and a few Chinese had sensed the failure of their country's institutions to meet the challenge. The door to change, while closed, had not been locked, and by 1895 the Sino-Japanese calamity pushed it ajar. Thereafter the cry for reform was never stilled, to the benefit of the Y.M.C.A. and other Western institutions. An atmosphere in which Western ideas could flourish had been created not only by military defeat but also by the gradual erosion of both Chinese and Western complacency. During the nineteenth century, Westerners in China were more inclined to teach than to learn. The events that remolded Chinese attitudes, however, for different reasons remolded Western responses as well.

One indication of an end to Western complacency was the

change in missionary attitudes. Western ideas came to China through many avenues, including the press and the experiences of Chinese students abroad. Every Westerner in China contributed his sprinkling of influence, be he trader, sailor, or diplomat. In large measure, however, Western social and intellectual ideas were at first transmitted most systematically by missionaries. Unfortunately nineteenth century missionaries often flaunted the banners of religious fanaticism and narrow nationalism. A few, though, learned through experience and generosity of spirit to develop communications with the Chinese, thereby creating a precedent for later secular groups. Missionary work was thus an indispensable prelude to the story of the Chinese Y.M.C.A. Two decades before the Association appeared in China, missionaries were already preparing the way.

The challenges of Western society were also creating new values and institutions within the United States itself. The men who went to China as Y.M.C.A. personnel represented a new breed, infused not only with a sense of service but also with qualities of practicality and flexibility. They were able to appreciate another culture, while at the same time remaining profoundly American in their values. Thus, the success of the Chinese Association was also rooted in American history.

The story unfolded simultaneously in many places. One location was Shanghai in the spring of 1877. On the morning of May 10, 1877, ninety-three male and female Protestant missionaries, along with assorted wives and guests, assembled in the lecture hall of the Temperance Society in Shanghai to hear the Reverend Dr. J. V. N. Talmage pray at length for "no more savage races, no barbarous tribes, no heathen idolatry." Thus opened officially the General Conference of the Protestant Missionaries of China.[1] Although in 1807 Robert Morrison

4

had gone to China as the first Protestant missionary, this was the first general missionary conference ever held in the country. In August 1874, missionaries of several denominations living or recuperating in the seaside city of Chefoo had unofficially attended a meeting of the Presbyterian Synod of China, at which a few participants, unintimidated by denominational rivalries, had suggested a national meeting.[2] Now, two and a half years later, missionaries from eight provinces had traveled to Shanghai by boat, sedan chair, and muleback to exchange ideas and take stock of their work.[3] When Dr. Talmage was finished praying, the conference members settled down to two weeks of controversy. After seventy years of existence, the Protestant movement in China appeared torn by dissension within and assailed by hostility without. For all the missionaries' work and prayer, the salvation of China seemed as remote as ever, and even some mildly revolutionary thinking was developing. As they assessed the aims, quality, and statistics of the missionary enterprise, a few participants concluded that the fault might lie less with the Chinese heathens than with the Westerners themselves.

The missionary movement between 1807 and the 1877 conference has been largely unexamined by historians, which leaves the period open to generalizations and stereotypes. Yet for all the diversity of men and works, one generalization is valid: the basic aim of Protestant missionaries in the nineteenth century was conversion. They had gone to China like soldiers, pledged to conquer the heathen for Christ or die gloriously in the attempt. Their memoirs report how they felt God call them personally from their farms in Wales or Pennsylvania, their villages in Georgia or coal mines in England. They sailed forth, armed with their Bibles, to preach the gospel message in which they believed so deeply: man was born to sin and would be forever damned unless he sought salvation through belief in Christ. The conversion of the Chinese, like their own, was to be conscious, unequivocal surrender to the imperatives of Christianity. Such conversion would probably be achieved only through great labor on the part of both missionary and heathen, but there was always the possibility that someone who heard even briefly the admonition of the Bible might be set on the road to salvation. To spread that message became the urgent and divine commandment of the missionaries. As a result, much communication with the Chinese took place on the religious level.[4]

This dedication to proselytizing overshadowed all other work. From the beginning missions maintained medical services and organized schools, but basically these services were intended only to make Christianity seem more attractive or to instruct children in religion while they were still pliable. The schools, almost all of which were confined to the primary level, generally offered a curriculum in which a Chinese instructor taught reading by rote in the morning, while the missionary and his assistant provided religious instruction in the afternoon.[5] Neither healing nor education was as important as preaching.

Thus, the first task of a denomination on arriving in a town was to raise a church where the Word might be proclaimed. Missionaries rented stores on busy thoroughfares to serve as chapels; they preached on the streets, at local fairs, in marketplaces, at scholarly examinations, in the tea shops—anywhere they were allowed. As soon as the Tientsin treaties of 1860 gave them the legal right to enter the interior, they began to travel by chair or mule to preach in outlying areas. Young Calvin Mateer roamed the countryside in the eighteen sixties carrying Bible tracts and a gun, with the cry of "devil" greeting him in every village.[6] In 1874 three men traveled eight hundred miles southwest from Peking to preach and distribute tracts.[7] The amount of energy per missionary expended on the Chinese soul was prodigious. They spared neither themselves nor their families, and it was not uncommon for a missionary to bury several wives and children while pursuing his work.[8] The 1877 report of the Shanghai and London Mission, by no means atypical, showed that of the four men who were members of the mission in China in 1855, one left from ill health in 1862, the second died in Hankow in 1863, the third returned home because of his wife's illness, and the fourth obtained a medical leave to Japan, where he died in 1865.[9] Mission board records speak delicately of men and women being sent to the seashore, to Japan, or home to the West to recuperate from breakdowns that were often mental. The toll was severe. Yet despite these expenditures of time, energy, courage, family, and life, the results that the 1877 conference could claim were meager.

Statistics offer one form of evidence for the missionaries' ineffectiveness. In the ten years between 1846 and 1856, four preachers of the American Board of Commissioners for Foreign Missions converted one Chinese at the Foochow station.[10] In the twenty-one years prior to 1866, the China Mission of the Southern Methodist Conference made from fifty to sixty conversions.[11] In subsequent years, after the treaties of Tientsin, the number of missionaries and the number of conversions grew, yet by 1877, a combined census of all Protestant affiliates showed only slightly more than 13,000 communicants to Protestant Christianity in China, representing the combined labors of 473 Western men and women besides an uncounted number of Chinese helpers. When compared with an estimated 400,000 Chinese Catholics, this number was not large; when compared with the hundreds of millions of Chinese infidels, it was appallingly small.[12] The "Christianization," meaning Protestantization, of the world petitioned for in Dr. Talmage's opening invocation to the 1877 conference was not yet in sight.

The identity of the Chinese Protestants further complicated the missionary problem. They clearly were not drawn from the influential upper classes of China, the official-scholar landholder "establishment" that controlled the country.[13] In fact, this group presented a virtually solid wall of indifference and hostility to Christianity.[14] Instead, the converted came primarily from the poor. The Methodist Episcopal Church in Foochow numbered in its congregation of 1858 a soldier, a day laborer, a basket maker, and one alleged member of the literati, their first convert claimed from that group.[15] In 1859, the Methodist Episcopal Church in Shanghai listed as its eleven members a widow, a dealer in precious stones and his wife, a carpenter, three button makers, a hatter, a teacher and his wife, and one man identified as a "scholar." However dedicated some of these people may have been, they were usually too poor to support the churches, and their influence in the community was restricted by their low social position.[16]

Furthermore, most of the Chinese Christians did not conform to the personal ideals of their Western saviors. Early missionaries admitted candidly that some of the converts were merely "rice Christians," willing to add another deity to their pantheon in return for a bowl of food. There were continual scandals about members who kept concubines or smoked opium or even gambled with church funds.[17] In Tungchow one church took care to pay out its money as quickly as it was acquired from the congregation so as not to accumulate a lump sum that might be lent out at interest, an activity long practiced by Chinese organizations that had acquired capital.[18] Old standards of Chinese behavior had survived conversion, though their persistence seemed unchristian to the Western missionary.

Just as distressing was the general apathy of Chinese Christians. The missionary eye had conjured up a kind of Chinese alter ego, one who, having been saved himself, would heed the call of God and roam the countryside preaching the Word. Christianity would race like an epidemic through the land; Christians would multiply and churches increase in a very contagion. Some day these churches would even be headed by the Chinese themselves, although in 1877 there was substantial agreement that the Chinese Christians were not yet sufficiently responsible to run their own congregations.[19] The key to this widespread conversion was expected to be the Chinese Christian, primarily the young Chinese Christian. Yet these very people, even the students in mission schools who were supposedly permeated by Christian influence, were often passive. Though nominally Christian, they showed no signs of taking up the battle against their own hostile pagan society.[20]

Only a supremely self-assured man could have convinced himself of eventual success when contemplating this record. But such men existed. Pearl Buck's father, Absalom Sydenstricker, never for a moment seemed shaken, so accoutered was he in his faith. Justus Doolittle, who was not alone in these convictions, once announced that the Chinese were "vile and deceptive and wicked beyond description," thus comfortably shifting the burden to Chinese shoulders.[21] Missionaries did not question their right to be in China, nor the universal truth of their message; instead, they attributed their lack of success, with some reason, to the hostility of the upper classes and the noncooperation of the Chinese government. In addition, they bemoaned their own lack of numbers. The 1877 conference passed a resolution to have a commission prepare a "fervid and earnest appeal" for reinforcements.[22]

A number of insurgents, however, appeared at the 1877 conference with new ideas. Among them were Calvin Mateer, Alexander Williamson, Joseph Edkins, Young J. Allen, John Nevius, and W. A. P. Martin—all having enough intellectual liveliness, imagination, and sympathy to blur the standard stereotype of the orthodox and narrow-minded preacher. These men bluntly placed much of the blame for the missionaries' lack of success on two factors in the movement itself: its quarrelsome sectarianism, and its insistence on preaching the gospel to the almost complete exclusion of other activities.

In 1877 there were already twenty-six different Protestant denominations represented in China: eleven American, thirteen British, and two from the Continent. Such a schism, charged Alexander Williamson on the second day of the conference, was "weakness and folly." The Chinese themselves were not particularly conscious of denominationalism, but the divisiveness meant both a lack of cooperation and a duplication of effort among the different sects. Much of the disunity reflected denominational pressures from home, since missionaries were supported by denominational boards, and a Methodist missionary was under pressure to produce a Chinese Methodist, not a Chinese Baptist. Doctrinal differences also occurred. For example, Pearl Buck's father, a Presbyterian, believed in baptizing converts by sprinkling their heads with water. The local Baptist missionary just as firmly believed in total immersion, claiming that the New Testament described Jesus as being submerged in the water. The two men, Miss Buck relates, fought bitterly over the question for thirty years. When the Baptist died, Mr. Sydenstricker remarked that he

10

"knew God would not allow this sort of thing to go on forever." [23]

Missionaries at the 1877 conference were aware of the lack of unity, but also aware of their dependence on home support. They appointed a Committee on the Division of Labor, which subsequently urged that different denominations working in the same region should try as far as possible to divide the territory and, when practical, to operate united schools and hospitals.[24] If the missionary effort could not actually be unified, however, it could perhaps be modified in other ways. Williamson and Mateer grumbled about denominationalism, but they saved their most persuasive words to advocate a different kind of program. Instead of preaching the gospel exclusively, they suggested, missionaries should adopt a broader intellectual approach through the schools and the press, for not the Word alone but knowledge as well was the key to the Chinese. Calvin Mateer, in a speech celebrated as the beginning of the intellectual movement among missionaries in China, urged the educators in the group to raise their academic standards.

Many of the missionaries, said Mateer, still opposed education because it was not directly related to the gospel. As a result, most missionary schools confined themselves to primary education and heavy religious instruction. It was true, he admitted, that Christianity and education were distinct, yet they had a strong affinity. Education was an agency for the truth, and missionary schools should carry on not only religious but also moral and mental education. If they provided knowledge of Western science and civilization, they could not fail to do good. China needed to be introduced to the science and arts of Western civilization, and if Christian men did not teach her, the infidels would.

Mateer therefore proposed that the missionaries establish advanced schools to teach geography, mathematics, history, science, and other Western secular subjects. He believed that such an undertaking was imperative for the future of Christianity in China, because the missionaries had to educate an effective native ministry, and ignorant men did not usually have influence in the country. Mateer added, "Almost all the intercourse which missionaries have with natives of the higher classes is dependent on the fact that they understand Western science and are qualified to speak of it." [25] Conversely, the missionaries' influence was small, he stated, because few of them knew anything about science.

Mateer was probing a sore spot. Seventy years after Robert Morrison had arrived in Canton as the first Protestant missionary to China, missionary relations with China's upper classes still ranged from nonexistent to hostile. Most missionaries agreed that this lack of communication with the upper classes seriously impeded their work, but a remedy did not appear at hand. There seemed little basis for cordiality. On political, ideological, cultural, and intellectual grounds, missionaries seemed to assault the upper classes, and the upper classes fought back.

To begin with, the missionary was branded with the stigma of imperialism. Until after the Opium War of 1840, he was confined to Canton with other Westerners, but as Western guns and treaties opened additional coastal cities to trade, the missionary followed the merchant. In 1860, after a combined French and English expedition had forced its way into Peking, treaties secured for Catholic and hence for Protestant missionaries the right to preach in the interior and to acquire land for homes and churches. Both Catholic and Protestant missionaries, therefore, were associated with the memory of violence.

12

Furthermore, the leader of the Taiping Rebellion, Hung Hsiu-ch'üan, used a distorted Christian framework for his appeal. Missionaries denounced the rebellion when they realized that its Christian elements were superficial, but it was not easy to disassociate themselves in Chinese minds from a man who claimed to be the younger brother of Jesus. After the rebellion was finally subdued in 1864, bitterness toward Christianity and thus toward missionaries persisted.

The antagonisms caused by national troubles were further exacerbated by a tug of war going on at the local level. The local elite or gentry, who supplied most of the aspirants for advancement into the literary degree-holding and official classes, had great power and prestige on the local scene and were traditionally the only nonofficial group with major influence. At the village level, where the national political structure did not formally reach, the gentry constituted a de facto government. As the missionary penetrated into the countryside, he knowingly or otherwise set himself up as a rival source of authority. He advised and protected his own converts, presented himself as the bearer of truth, and dealt with provincial and local officials as a social equal. Such invasion of privilege was not likely to win friends among the threatened class.[26]

It is axiomatic that hostility between two different types of people needs as a precondition neither political tension nor a power struggle. Strangeness is quite enough, and by almost any Chinese standard the missionary was strange. His short hair, his occidental features, his peculiar clothes, set him apart in a country almost totally innocent of foreigners. Westerners were called by names like "big nose," "barbarian," and "foreign devil." Such epithets were common; for instance, a man making every effort to be courteous to the missionary

Timothy Richard addressed him on one occasion as, "Your excellency the foreign devil." [27]

Furthermore, command of the Chinese language came slowly, if at all, to many missionaries. Generally they seem to have mastered the colloquial spoken Chinese, but to master the written classical Chinese was a huge task that few tackled successfully. Yet the star in the diadem of Chinese culture was its intricate, exquisite, exacting wen-li or classical language. Dominion over its subtleties marked the scholar; ignorance, the barbarian.

To all of these drawbacks the missionary often added another by vilifying Confucianism and the elite who were its guardians. James Legge, who became an eminent scholar of the classical language and admirer of the Confucian tradition, delivered a lecture at the 1877 conference maintaining that the Shang-ti mentioned in the classics was the same as the Christian God. By general agreement the essay was not even printed in the records of the conference because the proper Chinese term for God was so bitter a doctrinal question that the conference had agreed not even to discuss it. In the following months the pages of the missionary journal, *The Chinese Recorder,* were filled with passionate discussion of the essay. Significantly, one of the points made was the virtual heresy of comparing the Christian God with anything mentioned in the "vile Classics" of the Confucian tradition.[28] As late as 1890, when W. A. P. Martin stood before another general missionary conference and suggested tolerance on the subject of ancestor worship, almost the entire audience rose in protest.[29] Such denigration of the central tradition in Chinese society did not evoke affection from the upper classes.

The missionary's behavior was often mystifying as well. Why did he object to the Chinese pastimes of gambling, opium

14

smoking, and concubinage? Why did he behave like an inferior member of Chinese society, namely, a preacher? When a
missionary told Bible stories on a street corner or at a fair like
a public storyteller, he may have thought of himself as a
teacher, which was respectable, but to the Chinese he sounded
like a preacher, which was merely comical. What he preached
added to the mystery and the comedy. Although one cannot
generalize about the missionaries' message in China, they did
lay heavy emphasis on such non-Chinese concepts as original
sin, damnation, and redemption through worship of a cruci-
fied martyr. The Chinese reaction was varied. Listeners sometimes threw bricks; at other times they mimicked evangelical
performances in their own plays.[30] Occasionally they even
tolerated the message: an old woman once saved Absalom
Sydenstricker from harm by telling a crowd to listen respect-
fully, since he was trying to save his own soul.[31] The upper
classes did not themselves descend to brick throwing or ridi-
cule in the streets, although it has been convincingly suggested by one scholar that the gentry played an important part
behind the scenes in egging on the masses.[32] What the missionary generally encountered was indifference or inaccessibil-
ity. Upper class conversion was so rare that real exhilaration
occurred during the 1877 conference on hearing the rumor,
not necessarily accurate, that a *hsiu-ts'ai* or "first (lowest level)
degree holder" had become a Christian.[33] No one mistook this
for a trend.

The handful of men at the 1877 conference who pleaded for
a new approach, however, believed that at least the top
officials were becoming more accessible to an appeal on intellectual, if not on religious, grounds. From his eminence as
president of the Peking Interpreters' College (the T'ung-wen
Kuan or "School of Combined Learning"), which he had

headed by Chinese invitation since 1869, Martin spoke of a new intellectual movement in the country.[34] Calvin Mateer, who had pioneered as a science demonstrator, concluded that information on science was a good means, and possibly the only means, to reach the upper classes.

These and other missionaries were participating in a newly emerging trend in China toward active dissemination of Western knowledge. Before 1860 China had almost entirely ignored the importance of the West, refusing to initiate the study of mathematics, geography, and like subjects. In the 1860's, motivated by the invasion of the West, Li Hung-chang and other far-seeing Chinese officials had managed to establish language schools in Peking and Shanghai (1863), Canton (1864), and Foochow (1866). John Fryer, for example, first taught English at the Peking school, then taught French and served as a translator at the Shanghai school after it was put under the administration of the new Kiangnan Arsenal. Other Westerners, many of them missionaries, also functioned as school principals and faculty in these schools. The language schools, like several schools later established to teach engineering, telegraphy, medicine, mining, and naval affairs, lay outside the periphery of proper Chinese education, but they represented a genuine breach in China's wall of indifference to Western learning. Another such breach was provided by the famous educational mission of Yung Wing, who brought one hundred and twenty Chinese boys to study in Connecticut between 1872 and 1881. By no means all of the Westerners who shared in these experiments were missionaries, but by their very availability, missionaries played a major role.

It was on this growing interest in the scientific and technical achievements of the West that Mateer wanted to capitalize. He himself was daily piling up evidence of Chinese interest in science. Mateer, a Presbyterian minister, had brought to China not only a theological background but also a college training in science. Assigned to found a school at Tengchow (later Tengchow College), on the coast of Shantung Province, he soon began to teach science to his theology students with the help of equipment sent him by American supporters. He therefore knew from his own experience that the Chinese were interested in Western technology. In 1874 he gave a chemistry demonstration in the city of Chefoo, using as his assistant the newly arrived Welsh Baptist Timothy Richard, who later credited Mateer with being the father of modern science education in China.[35]

Backing up Mateer's experiment at the Tengchow school was an extraordinary piece of evidence from the past. Mateer and his fellow-insurgents were aware that three hundred years earlier the Jesuit pioneers had used scientific demonstrations to win the attention and then the respect of many Chinese officials and literati.[36] Matthew Ricci, gifted as a mathematician and astronomer, had made sundials and maps, corrected the Chinese calendar, lectured on science, and even tinkered with some of the clocks he had presented to influential officials.[37] His work and that of his successors had faded from official Chinese memory, but the West did not forget, and in 1877 Protestant missionaries were thoughtfully reviewing the Jesuit experience.

To Mateer's urging at the 1877 conference of formal science instruction through the natural channel of the schools, Alexander Williamson added the suggestion of disseminating not only scientific but also general information about the West through some form of missionary publishing venture. But to many at the conference, such suggestions had little to do with the real work of spreading the gospel. To Mateer's plea for advanced schools teaching secular and scientific courses, Dr. Talmage expressed the fear that Christianity might be looked upon as merely an outgrowth of education. Devello Z. Sheffield, founder of the Tungchow Boys' School of the American Board, agreed with him, and Dr. R. Nelson from the American Protestant Episcopal Mission in Shanghai warned that literary labor could not be accounted full consecration to the work of seeking souls for Christ. When Williamson quoted the maxim that the press ruled the world, J. Hudson Taylor of the China Inland Mission retorted, "Brethren, the Lord Jesus rules the world!" [38]

Despite these caveats, conference members decided to make a modest start in the direction of intellectual improvement. They appointed a committee on literature to find out what books already published by missionaries could be used generally and to secure preparation of a suitable series for schools, including books on arithmetic, geography, astronomy, and natural philosophy. They recommended that Martin, Williamson, Mateer, Fryer, Young J. Allen, and John Lechler form a committee to prepare a series of schoolbooks. In the following months this committee recommended two series, one for primary and one for advanced schools, both written in the simplest wen-li or classical language, and both emphasizing science. John Fryer further encouraged the movement by announcing that the directors of the Kiangnan Arsenal would cut the whole series on blocks and print them at cost if they contained nothing objectionable to the Chinese.[39]

The conference took no steps toward forming a unified, advanced school system, but after the meeting various denominations began to develop colleges, or at least institutions called colleges, which corresponded to advanced schools in the West. The Methodist Episcopal Mission planned colleges for

Foochow, Kiukiang, and Peking, and an enthusiastic American Board member in Tientsin, Charles Stanley, began to agitate for a secular college in that city. From this literary and academic seed there later grew an impressive system.

But there were other bonds that could be forged with the Chinese, and at least two missionaries, Timothy Richard and Gilbert Reid, were trying a different approach to them. During the Shanghai conference, Richard was in the interior experimenting with new methods of communication. A remarkable and independent man, he arrived in Chefoo from Wales in 1870 and, like other missionaries, set to preaching in street chapels. After more than two years of fruitless effort, he became disgusted by his lack of success and by the competition of a large number of missionaries for a few converts.[40] He concluded, "if God had really called me to be a missionary, he would at the same time have prepared some of the Chinese to hear my message." [41] If there were no such listeners in Chefoo, they must exist elsewhere. Accordingly, he decided to ride out of the city into the interior and to follow the plan of "seeking the worthy." [42] Thus began a pilgrimage into the country villages, to Tsinan and Tsingchow in Shantung, and eventually to Shansi, seeking anyone who would listen to his message.

Richard first found his "worthy" among the hospitably eclectic adherents of the folk religions. Members of the local sects, Buddhist priests, and later even officials were willing to listen to him. His early approach was not didactic. One technique was the science lecture. By the time that Richard assisted Calvin Mateer in the Chefoo science demonstration, he himself had already begun to train his own Chinese assistants in physics and chemistry, in order to combat the Chinese superstition he discovered around him. He studied the Jesuit records and spent a sizable legacy on scientific equipment. Much later, in 1881, he began to lecture on scientific subjects in Taiyuan, in Shansi Province, at the specific request of officials and scholars.[43] That this was entirely compatible with his missionary calling he did not doubt. Richard was basically a product of the Enlightenment, which in one aspect saw science as an important manifestation of God's laws. Science lectures might convince the Chinese that nature was only God's Word made flesh.

Thus Richard and Mateer were agreed on the importance of science. But since Richard did not operate within the confines of a missionary school with an essentially captive audience, he had to build his own bond with the Chinese. It was not at first through science that he fashioned this bond, but through a strenuous effort to meet the Chinese on their own terms, much as Matthew Ricci had done. Science linked these two men from different centuries, cultures, and persuasions, but they were also linked by a respect for the Chinese and an acceptance of many Chinese values. Ricci had adopted the dress and social customs of the Chinese literati. One entry in his diary, for example, speaks of his donning a scholar's silk robe and hat and riding in a sedan chair accompanied by the proper number of servants to call on a high official. At another time he mentions blushing in the appropriate manner when an official complimented him.[44] His intellectual gifts were extraordinary; his command of written characters was such that he could rapidly scan a random selection of characters, immediately repeat them in order, and then repeat them backwards, a demonstration of learning and showmanship that dazzled his audience. His grasp of the language went far beyond mere tricks, however, extending to the writing of books in Chinese, which established him as a scholar. All these accomplishments and niceties of behavior marked Ricci as a man of breeding, rather than an ill-mannered barbarian.

Timothy Richard, too, adjusted himself to the values of the upper classes whenever possible. Like Ricci, he became a fine language scholar and author. Again like Ricci, he tried to conform to proper etiquette, as in the question of hair styles. The Chinese had worn a queue as symbol of their submission to the Manchus for so long that it had become customary and therefore correct. One day in Tsingchow, Richard put on a Chinese gown, shaved his head, and affixed an artificial queue. Walking down the street, he heard someone exclaim, "Ah, now he looks like a man!" That very afternoon he received an invitation to tea from a hitherto inaccessible official, who blandly explained that before then, Richard had looked so peculiar in his Western clothes and Western hair style that curious crowds would have ripped the paper windows of the house to get a look at him.[45]

Richard learned his lesson well. In 1875, when the T'ung-chih emperor died, he went unshaven in accordance with Chinese custom. When he lectured to the upper classes of Taiyuan, he always carefully separated his audiences by rank, to indicate his acceptance of the social structure.[46] But even more important than his good manners were his good works. He spent days with one official, helping him to break the opium habit; he gave freely of his quinine during a malaria epidemic; he started an orphanage and converted it into an industrial school. Wherever he turned, he was useful, and his basic motivation was human concern more than conversion. What most earned him Chinese affection and gratitude, however, was his work in North China between 1876 and 1878 organizing famine relief.

During those years North China was almost rainless. When famine first crept into Shantung in 1876, Richard rode out through the countryside to investigate and help. After his early attempts to administer personal relief met with near disaster because of the mobs and the officials' fear that he was trying to incite rebellion, he organized a plan involving Chinese-Western cooperation. His plea to missionaries resulted in an outpouring of funds, and he succeeded in enlisting the help of the Chinese themselves. Gentry from Kiangsu Province, he wrote, agreed to administer the funds, and the Shantung native bankers distributed cash "honestly and promptly." [47]

In 1877 when famine struck the inland province of Shansi, Richard rode there to find an even worse situation. Women were being carried off in carts to be sold; people fell dead as they tottered along the streets; wild dogs ate corpses; and a whisper of cannibalism was heard. Here, too, Richard successfully canvassed both Westerners and Chinese for help. This time he worked with Tseng Kuo-ch'uan, younger brother of the general Tseng Kuo-fan, and with the eminent Li Hung-chang. His experiences led him to decide that, despite what he had heard from colleagues, members of the Chinese upper classes were often fine men.[48] His subsequent history indicates that the appreciation was mutual. Li Hung-chang listened to his recommendations on Chinese problems with respect; Chang Chih-tung, governor of Shansi, asked him to enter the Chinese service; and the gentry of Taiyuan requested that he educate their sons. As a reward for his eclecticism, he was subsequently hounded out of Shansi by his colleagues on charges of heresy and became editor of the Tientsin newspaper *Shih-pao* (The Times) for Li Hung-chang. As time passed, he concentrated most of his energies on journalism. In 1891 he became head of the Society for Diffusion of Christian and General Knowledge

(SDK), the missionary general publishing venture that had grown from the 1877 committee on textbooks and was headed by Alexander Williamson until his death in 1890. Richard's interest in science did not flag; in 1887 he persuaded a former colleague, J. S. Whitewright, to found a small science museum in Tsingchow. Along with this concentration on science and literature, Richard reaffirmed his belief that the means to influence China was through her upper classes. "If you get the leaders," he remarked, "you get all the rest." [49]

The American Presbyterian Gilbert Reid was beginning to reach similar conclusions. Reid collaborated with Richard in the Shansi famine relief program in 1877 and worked in cooperation with the Shansi gentry. He, like Richard, became convinced that the key to changing China lay with its upper classes. If the Chinese mandarin could not be made a convert, Reid declared to the Presbyterians of Shantung in November 1887, he could at least be made a friend. The way to accomplish this was to offer friendship. Any approach would be helpful: medical work, scientific lectures, general education. He added that the best method was not to concentrate on the poor but to start as high as possible and work down. It was all very well to argue, as some did, that Christ started at the bottom. But Henry Stanley of Africa had adopted another approach. If you wanted to settle in the Congo, he advised, secure an introduction to the emperor. In consequence, Reid adopted Chinese dress, studied Chinese etiquette, and applied himself to the task of meeting influential Chinese, though with little luck. In 1888 he got the chance to make such contacts in Peking itself, where he had gone the previous December to seek help from the American ministry in protecting missionary property. When he learned that he might be detained for several months, Reid moved into a Chinese temple with nothing foreign in his possession but a few books. He memorized the classics, learned the official ranks and personages of the central government, prepared documents on reform, and tried to pay calls on highly placed officials. Although only three acknowledged him, Reid remained confident that with time, money, and tact the influential men of the capital could be reached.[50]

Thus, in the last years of the nineteenth century a change was in the making. Most missionaries still concentrated on the gospel, but a start was underway toward enlarging the intellectual dimensions of the missionary movement. Richard and Reid were summoning an even broader vision of the ways in which men from one culture could bridge the gap with those from another. They were groping toward a concept of a mission toward the whole man—as a mind to be taught, a human being to be fed, a personality to be enjoyed, as well as a soul to be saved. They were increasingly dedicated to involving the leaders of Chinese society in this enterprise. An articulate new voice in Sino-Western communication, they pointed the way to a redefinition of the missionary's task. It soon became apparent that they were not alone.

2

YOUTH AND THE Y.M.C.A.

Reinforcement for the Richard–Reid philosophy came, paradoxically, from deep within the gospel tradition. In the years immediately following the 1877 conference, most missionaries clung to the conviction that preaching the gospel was their most important and effective work. Although literary and educational efforts promised higher intellectual standards and a chance to establish communication with the upper classes, these rewards would come in the future, if indeed they came at all. For the present, the most promising field of activity lay not among the upper but among the lower classes; the real task was not nourishing minds but saving souls, and the Chinese Christian soul itself appeared in continuing need of improvement, for even within the mission schools, religious commitment languished. The non-Christian student usually used the schools merely to acquire knowledge of English and arithmetic, which would help in getting a job with foreign businessmen. Christian students were not exempt from these temptations. Thus, to many a missionary laboring to raise a healthy crop of Christians, science laboratories or mathematics courses appeared not only irrelevant but downright dangerous. D. Z. Sheffield of the Tungchow Boys' School had pointed out at the 1877 conference that "secular education did not of itself bring men nearer to Christ." [1] Missionaries hardly cared to educate young Chinese as modern men and Christians only to have them keep the modernity and slough off the Christianity. Ignorance might be regrettable, but apathy was deplorable.

Apathy is a relative term. For men with the zeal of, say, the Reverend Dr. Talmage or J. Hudson Taylor, anything short of the boiling point might have seemed tepid. Still, the missionaries by no means wholly misjudged their flocks, for Chinese Christian students were indeed apathetic. In part this derived from their defensiveness in a hostile society; in part it came from the heavy diet of religious instruction set before them each day by men who were sometimes better theologians than teachers. The passivity of the young was also encouraged by the Chinese tradition of obedience, not only to a father but to an entire network of authority figures who were either older or higher in the social scale or more advanced in the family hierarchy. Young people were not supposed to think independently. Their fathers or other elders made the decisions; custom and law reinforced a young man's duty to accept those decisions. Authoritarianism bred passivity, at least outwardly, and the modulation from passivity to apathy was not difficult. Extended to the classroom, the tradition produced docile students, but it was not likely to develop flaming evangelists.[2]

By the mid-1880's, however, there were some young missionaries in China whose religious enthusiasm had been encouraged by a new approach adopted when they themselves were students. This approach postulated a generally more optimistic and joyful Christianity than the version brought to China by the older Protestant missionaries. Furthermore, the approach operated on the principle that nothing bred enthusiasm as much as personal responsibility and participation. To determine whether religious enthusiasm could be similarly encouraged in China, missionaries in two schools turned over some of the responsibility for the Chinese soul to the Chinese themselves; specifically, to the Chinese student.

The program began modestly. One day in 1885, reports a memoir written fifty years later, an American Presbyterian missionary appeared at the Anglo-Chinese College of the Methodist Episcopal Mission at Foochow and suggested to the principal, George Smyth, that the Christian students organize a young men's group. By doing religious work personally instead of merely being exposed to it, they might develop their own spiritual natures and at the same time learn to serve others. Within a month Smyth persuaded forty-five students to form an organization called the Yu-t'u hui or Young Disciples' Association—their translation of the English title Young Men's Christian Association. The Association was simply a daily prayer group. Every weekday afternoon at four o'clock the members assembled for a religious meeting. What made this in any way distinctive was that the students led the meetings themselves, and that one of their number, Ch'en Meng-jen, was elected president. In this way the students became active participants in the religious ritual. So successful was the technique, the writer recalled, that after two years membership increased markedly, and some students plucked up enough courage and pride in their Christianity to start preaching the gospel off-campus, just as the missionaries themselves did.[3]

Near Peking, in the Tungchow Boys' School of the American Board, the same pattern was developing under the influence of Harlan Beach, who had come to the school as a teacher via Yale and Andover Theological Seminary. By 1885 the American Board in North China was reevaluating the whole problem of education versus the gospel. D. Z. Sheffield, who had taken an anti-intellectual stand in 1877 despite his own academic eminence, had modified his position and was proposing to turn the Tungchow Boys' School into a respectable college.[4] His young colleague Beach advocated genuine education, aimed at making his students think rather than merely parrot their lessons. But at the same time Beach wanted to nourish spiritual excellence, to develop in his students the kind of active religious enthusiasm he himself felt. Within him kindled the hope "of fostering in them the desire to contribute somewhat in their undergraduate life to the evangelization of this city and its immediate neighborhood." [5]

Beach had seen just such a desire stirred in American college students through their fellowship in the college branch of the Young Men's Christian Association. These college Associations emphasized a nonritualistic, joyful religious experience, and they were run by the students themselves. Before coming to China, Beach had promised the secretary of the college Associations in the United States that he would try to start a similar group in Tungchow. In 1885 his first attempt met with failure, but by 1886 he had persuaded the students to start a group. The success was gratifying. Soon the students installed a fellow-student, Ch'uan Wen-shou, as president, and began to serve as lay preachers. They conducted prayer meetings not only for themselves but also for non-Christian students. Each Sunday afternoon student teams traveled to nearby villages to preach the gospel, and they began to hold evening meetings to try to reach businessmen unavailable in the daytime. They even contributed funds to help educate a Zulu student in Natal to do Christian work. New conversions were as scarce as ever, but Beach wrote home that the students themselves were already learning "the luxury of doing good." Far from being passive, they had quickly taken over the real leadership of the Association. In Beach's eyes, the new Association promised much for the future, since it could teach his students, many of whom were prospective pastors, the practice rather than merely the theory of Christian work.[6] By 1888 he wrote that a new spirit had come over the school since the founding of the Association.[7]

The Foochow and Tungchow experiments were only a weak echo of a loud new theme in American Protestantism. By the

1880's thousands of American students were moving off their cloistered campuses to carry on lay religious work in mountain villages, city jails, almshouses, docks, and streets. They had been seized by the conviction that they shared a religious responsibility for souls other than their own, and this sense of domestic missionary urgency was matched by the optimistic belief that the young, particularly students, could exert a powerful influence on others. The students' missionary fervor was part of a much more extensive phenomenon in the United States. The Protestant layman had come to believe that he held not only a special spiritual power but also a unique social responsibility. This belief, embodied in the Social Gospel, was gradually broadening the task of Protestant Christianity to include many aspects of life besides personal spiritual salvation.

One of the most vigorous expressions of this new sentiment was the Young Men's Christian Association, familiarly termed the Y.M.C.A. or "Y." It had started in England as an organization not for students but for clerks. By the middle of the nineteenth century the irresistible tide of the Industrial Revolution had washed into dark Liverpool shops and crowded London offices thousands of country boys who wished to make their way as apprentices. George Williams, a Somerset farm boy who worked long hours in a London dry goods firm and shared cramped quarters in the firm's dormitory, became disturbed by the quality of life led by his young associates and himself. He felt that their existence was starved of meaning and stimulation, that they lived in an intellectual and spiritual vacuum, with only the doubtful and expensive temptations of the city to offer relief. Williams was an ardent Christian who found sustenance in his faith. In 1841 he therefore joined with eleven other young men of various Protestant persuasions to form a group that met every night for prayer and medita-

tion. Soon the group acquired more members, together with
meeting rooms, a small library, the benign approval of the
firm's head, and the name Young Men's Christian Association.
To prayer was added self-improvement in the form of practical
classes and lectures. By 1851 similar groups existed in seventeen cities in Great Britain and Ireland, and the general philosophy of the Association began to crystallize. Membership was
open to all young men. The Association was Christian in
spirit, but interdenominational and run by laymen. Its general
purpose was the improvement of young men.[8]

The idea swiftly proved sturdy enough to thrive across the
Atlantic. In 1851 Associations were started in Montreal and
Boston, and four years later there were forty-nine city groups
on the American continent, linked by a rudimentary regional
and national organization. The city Associations were paralleled in the late 1850's by a few scattered Associations on
college campuses, which, however, were overshadowed by
their city counterparts. In the period before the Civil War,
Y.M.C.A. denoted the bustling, practical city Associations, dis-
tinctively American in values, who ambitiously declared their
goal to be "the improvement of the spiritual, mental, social
and physical condition of young men." [9]

There had been other youth groups in America before the
Y.M.C.A. idea was imported, but they were not notably successful. Some were too exclusively linked to denominational
religious worship; others were so secular that they could not
gain the powerful backing of the Protestant clergy; several
were poorly organized or badly financed.[10] The Y.M.C.A. sur-
mounted all of these obstacles. It evolved a useful program for
urbanizing America, a pervasive but not asphyxiating religious
atmosphere, and an awesome knack for raising money. It
suited the temper of the times.

The Y.M.C.A. matched the optimistic atmosphere of nine-

teenth-century American society with its own optimistic assumptions about the nature of man. He might, as the Bible
taught, be basically sinful, but he was also basically teachable.
His mind, body, and character could be properly molded by
suitable education and activity. The end result would be a
healthy, skilled young man with the training to make his own
way in society and a sense of values that would obligate him to
help others to do the same. He would be, in the large sense of
the term, a Christian gentleman. If he met his duties to
himself, to his community, and to his God, the reward would
be success in this world and salvation in the next.

The program shaped by this philosophy gained ready acceptance, for the city Y.M.C.A. provided a specific and often
effective answer to many problems besetting middle class
America at mid-century. The United States, like England, was
making an awkward adjustment to the Industrial Revolution.
Much has been written about the plight of the European
immigrants who poured into American cities during the middle of the nineteenth century. To a lesser degree, the city also
represented a strange and hostile environment to many na-
tive-born Americans. As a result of the changing economic
patterns brought on by industrialization, farm boys migrated
to the cities looking for better economic opportunities. They,
like the European immigrants, stepped into a society with a
different pace and values from their own. The city offered
more economic opportunity than a marginal farm, but it demanded new skills and greater competitiveness. The gaiety of
city life often clashed with the mores of rural America. And
the city could be lonely.[11]

The plight of the migrant from a farm thirty miles away
could not compare with the problems of an immigrant from
Europe, but the country boy, too, needed a job, a place to live,

an anchor for his values, and friends. In these areas and others, the Y.M.C.A. adapted the English model to the American scene. A group of laymen in a city would form an Association, rent rooms, and begin to provide services that they thought were useful and proper for young strangers to the city. The pioneer Boston Association, for example, operated for a few years in rented quarters and then, after a spirited financial campaign, in a building of its own. It actively solicited membership by means such as posting notices in the railroad station and notifying all Protestant clergymen within a fifty-mile radius that boys coming into the city could use its facilities. The Boston Association listed approved boarding houses, started an employment bureau, opened a reading room, ran lecture series, carried on Bible classes, and operated a night school. Its library catalog for 1874 shows that the 4,250-volume library was stocked not only with religious tracts but also with such diverse fare as De Quincey's "Confessions of an Opium-Eater," an algebra text, an exposé of the Mormons, the works of Coleridge, and a book by one Thomas A. Davis entitled *How To Make Money and How To Keep It*.[12] Associations gave teas and picnics, held fairs, arranged riverboat outings, and conducted social hours with suitable young ladies. In 1856 the New York Association acquired a gymnasium and began an athletic program. The Y.M.C.A., in other words, provided practical answers to the personal and professional problems of the young men it attracted.

Members, however, were not supposed to be passive recipients of help. Flowing from the idea that Christian responsibility included service by the community at large to its young men was the corollary conviction that in return those young men owed some service to the community. Thus, city Associations from the start carried on humanitarian work. In cold weather they distributed coal and clothing. During the New Orleans yellow fever epidemic of 1858 the local group set up a citywide relief system. During the Civil War, Associations carried on work in prison hospitals, in the field, and among the troops. Such work was particularly noteworthy in an age that relegated relief to private agencies.[13]

The idea of community service grew directly from the religious convictions of the organization. The Association was by no means a church, however. Young men of any religious persuasion, or none, were welcome to join without subscribing to the tenets of Protestant Christianity, although they could not vote on Association affairs unless they were members of one of the evangelical churches—a policy reached partly out of piety and partly out of desire for the support of those powerful churches. Yet the Association was indisputably permeated by the Protestant Christian spirit, with the overtones of evangelical activism implied by that spirit. It was inevitable that along with demonstrating Christianity in action, Associations should also begin to preach Christianity.

In the autumn of 1856 several members of the New York Y.M.C.A. started noontime prayer meetings in the Wall Street financial area to appeal to young men in the vicinity who did not ordinarily go to church. Lay members of the Association led short, interdenominational, spontaneous prayers that emphasized faith rather than doctrine. At first the meetings went unnoticed, but when a severe financial panic hit the country the following August, attendance began to soar. The newspapers took note. Association members commandeered churches and meeting halls elsewhere in the city for similar meetings, which also were rapidly crowded. From New York to San Francisco a spirit of intense revivalist enthusiasm erupted as

Y.M.C.A. members began to hold meetings in churches, halls, and even in a "prayer tent" on the Boston Common. As the "Great Revival" spread, new city Associations were established, and the shock waves from the religious explosion generated many college Y.M.C.A.'s. The revival demonstrated compellingly both to the evangelical churches and to Protestants as a whole the power of the layman and the appeal of this new approach to religion. After the initial wave of enthusiasm subsided, the Association found that its religious work, coupled with its practical work, had made it indisputably the most popular and successful young men's group in the country. By 1860 there were 205 active city Associations, loosely headed by what was called the International Committee.[14] After the Civil War, Associations sprang up throughout the country.

Such success demanded not only a program but also proper organization and financing. The Association developed a system of paid staff called "secretaries," whose personalities were keys to the organization's success. Y.M.C.A. secretaries were doers. As one of them wrote, he had initially been attracted to the job because the city Associations seemed to call for "talents ordinarily relegated to business, engineering and statecraft." [15] An embodiment of such talent was the first full-time paid secretary, John Wanamaker, who subsequently became head of his own department store empire. American secretaries were effective building consultants, educators, athletic directors, relief organizers, and fund raisers, sometimes concurrently. Their executive talents in the fund raising field were essential, for the Y.M.C.A. operated on the assumption that each city Association would rely on local support. Apart from membership fees, most financing came in the shape of contributions from the business community, and some secretaries were geniuses at extracting money from local businessmen.

The most successful Y.M.C.A. fund raiser of his time was an extraordinary man named Dwight Lyman Moody.[16] Serving briefly as an officer but principally as a volunteer, he embodied the spirit, vitality, and optimism of the Association to such a degree that to many people he became known as "Mr. Y.M.C.A." Dwight Moody was born in 1837 in that nursery of revivalism, western Massachusetts. A fatherless, impoverished farm boy with the barest education, he was sent to Boston to seek his fortune but soon removed himself to the bustling city of Chicago, a decade before the Civil War. There Moody proceeded to become an outstandingly successful shoe jobber. But a sense of religious vocation nurtured in his childhood continued to pursue him. When the Great Revival reached Chicago, Moody decided to serve as a Bible teacher. He accordingly plunged into the slums and began to hunt out not only the sailors and drunks who frequented the area, but also the young ragamuffins who swarmed the streets of "Little Hell." At his own expense he brought these children to makeshift rooms, fed them, clothed them, and preached to them. Since Moody radiated an intense personal magnetism as well as providing material attractions, not only children but their parents, and shortly the prosperous middle class residents of the city, began to clamor to hear him. By the Civil War he had become famous in Chicago as a revivalist. A member of the Y.M.C.A. since his Boston days, he rapidly became the most enthusiastic and effective member of the Chicago Association.

Both Moody's brand of religion and his form of presentation were refreshing to his audiences. For one thing, he brought a new optimism to his preaching. American Protestants were conditioned to hear that they were in disrepute with God. Over a hundred years before, the zealous Jonathan Edwards had preached a sermon called "Sinners in the Hands of an Angry God," which reportedly drove a four-year-old mad with fear. On the frontier at the turn of the nineteenth century, itinerant Methodist circuit riders—preachers on horseback—bellowed of sin and damnation to their audiences at camp meetings. In the 1850's, the revivalist Charles Finney, although somewhat less grim, sent whole villages into paroxysms of terror.[17] It was this chilling tradition that had been exported to the Orient. Moody was of a different sort. "God does not love sin," he informed his audiences, "but he loves men in their sin." "I earnestly believe," he wrote, "that God is love." To his associates he confided, "There is nothing like keeping the people stirred up all the time, full of courage—full of hope." [18] This attitude appealed to his audiences. Equally attractive was Moody's insistence on the universality of Christianity. He overrode creeds, doctrines, and denominations. The God encountered through Moody's influence was considerably more hospitable than the one his listeners had come to know as youngsters.

This comforting doctrine was delivered in a disarming manner. Moody was, to say the least, nonintellectual. Theology did not interest him because he could not understand doctrinal quibbles. Long involved prayers did not appeal to him because, as he quipped, "when a man is making one, very likely the people are praying he will stop." [19] Instead, he stood before his audience, plump, bewhiskered, friendly, practical, and read the Bible aloud. When he came to a word he did not understand, he just skipped it and kept going. His colleague Ira

Sankey would lift his melodious voice in a hymn; Moody would deliver a warm, hopeful sermon. The response of the audience was tremendous.

Moody soon abandoned his business career to spend the rest of his life as a religious revivalist, and the ties he had forged with the Y.M.C.A. gradually became firmer. He turned his prodigious money-raising energies toward putting the local Association on a solvent basis, and in 1865 he became President of the Chicago group. His bubbling optimism, his homely wit, his financial acumen, his genuine goodness of heart, made him strike many people as the embodiment of the Association ideal: a farm boy who had gone to the city, succeeded in business, shared his fortune with others, and remained an ardent Christian.[20] It was indirectly through his influence that the spirit of the city Associations finally reached the colleges of the country.

By 1874 there were only thirty-four college Associations in the United States. Some provided a number of student services similar to those of the city Associations, but their main emphasis was usually evangelical. At the University of Virginia, for example, students went into the surrounding mountain hamlets to serve as lay preachers. Unlike most other college religious societies, the student Y.M.C.A.'s thus had some contact with life beyond the campus. The college Associations were not joined to one another, but they did send delegations to the city Association conventions and maintained a link with the national movement. It was through such means that the spirit of untutored Dwight Moody reached Princeton.

In 1875 an Indiana farm boy named Luther Wishard transferred from Hanover College to Princeton to prepare himself for the ministry.[21] Wishard's religious enthusiasm had first been stirred by hearing his father describe a convention at which Moody had spoken, and it was permanently aroused by his own evangelical work in the Hanover Y.M.C.A. He went to Princeton profoundly convinced that for the college student there were spiritual obligations and rewards outside the campus. Princeton in particular, he felt, could leaven its aloofness and clannishness by more contact with the community. Wishard was a mystic, but also an organizer of enormous vigor. In 1876 he persuaded the Princeton student religious society, called the Philadelphian Society, to become a student Y.M.C.A. He then induced other student Associations to form an intercollegiate student network, and ultimately brought the student network into the formal structure of the federated city Associations. The student Associations were thus caught up in the favorite American ritual of regional and national conventions. In 1879 Dwight Moody presided at a Baltimore student conference. Thereafter, student Associations were regularly visited by Moody, by local laymen, and by missionaries on home leave from abroad, and Moody began to take an increasing interest in the development of student work.

Wishard had initially set out to study for the ministry, influenced and buoyed in this hope by his Princeton roommate Robert Mateer, who was Calvin Mateer's brother and who was himself planning to go to China. Wishard, too, dreamed of a career as a China missionary. But as his student Association grew into a reality, he became more deeply immersed in student work, and in 1877 he abandoned the idea of a missionary career to become the first formal secretary of the intercollegiate Y.M.C.A., which he himself had created. His missionary zeal, however, did not disappear. One day he learned that the first American foreign mission agency, the American Board of Commissioners for Foreign Missions, had been organized in 1810 as the result of a plea by several Williams

College students. These students had taken refuge in a haystack on a stormy day in 1806 and had there shared a vision of sending an outpouring of students abroad as missionaries. Their influence had led to the formation of the American Board, although their further dream of organizing an intercollegiate missionary movement had come to nothing at the time. Wishard was electrified by the story of the "Men of the Haystack," as they were called, and by the special power he therefore detected in students to bring about the salvation of the world.[22] He decided to carry on their work. For this reason he entered a plea for student missionaries at the Baltimore student meeting of 1879 over which Moody presided, and from that time on the two men combined their energies to encourage a student missionary movement. In Canada and the United States, college Associations that had caught Wishard's enthusiasm initiated missionary societies—notably at Princeton in 1883. Moreover, Wishard dreamed of establishing a world network of student Christian Associations, in which students of other countries could demonstrate the same religious fervor and responsibility now manifest on American campuses. He began to extract from Association members going overseas as missionaries, among them Harlan Beach, the promise to start informal student Associations wherever they could.[23]

It was thus the religious vigor of the American student Y.M.C.A. that first propelled the Association idea overseas as a prayer movement, and which was responsible for the Foochow and Tungchow experiments. However, the more mundane ideas of the city Associations were already spreading to Asia. In Bombay the Association started a coffee shop and an athletic program; a missionary in India asked that several well-trained men be sent there as regular city Association secretaries. In Tokyo, John Swift, an Association secretary originally sent by Moody and Wishard to teach English and to work with existing student groups, donated a personal inheritance of twenty-five thousand dollars for a building where city work could be carried on. In 1887 an American secretary from Pittsburgh wrote an article for the Y.M.C.A.'s official publication, *The Watchman*, proposing expansion of the city movement abroad.[24] Given the Association concept of the whole man, it was natural that along with its religious ideals, the other aspects of the Association should move toward the Orient.

During these years the idea of a formally sponsored Association in China was being encouraged by Harlan Beach. In 1885 he actually made a few inquiries about bringing a number of American laymen to China to do religious work with his students, on which subject he conducted an inconclusive correspondence with Wishard.[25] Although the idea got nowhere, Beach did not abandon his faith in the lay worker. Trained seminary graduates, he felt, would be ideal for China once the middle and upper classes had opened themselves to Christian preaching. "But for now," he declared, "when only the poor and despised of China are heeding the Gospel call, the lay worker with Y.M.C.A. experience will not only be as useful but even more useful than the seminary graduate." At the Tungchow station, most of the effective work was being done neither by foreigners nor by their trained helpers, but by the chapel keeper, who was a "typical Y.M.C.A. man." China needed his nonintellectual, warm approach, Beach was convinced, for "in this land *touch* and not the *word* moves the heart." The advantages of the Y.M.C.A. man were numerous: "The Y man has been trained in the school of versatility, we in that of routine and fixedness. He knows the Bible, we our

Systematic Theology. He is a simple minded man with nothing in himself to trust in, while we unconsciously rely on our education and rhetoric . . . The Y man trusts in God and brings down his man." [26] Beach's belief in the Association idea and the Association personality grew steadily. But he, like Mateer and Richard and many others before him, was coming to realize that gospel preaching, even Association gospel preaching, was not capturing the imagination of the Chinese. Student preaching might be improving the students' souls, but it was not making converts. He therefore instituted a lecture program on science and began to show Bible scenes on the new stereopticon. Both programs proved great attractions.[27] Thus, even in this bastion of the pure gospel, the recreational and educational ideals of the city Association began to make inroads.

Meanwhile, Wishard's organizations were multiplying. In 1886 he persuaded Dwight Moody to open the campus of Moody's new school in Northfield, Massachusetts, for a summer conference of Y.M.C.A. members, which combined athletics, music, and prayer. Speakers included Dr. William Ashmore, a missionary from China, and Dr. A. T. Pierson, a mission promoter who called for "the evangelization of the world in this generation." [28] In the charged atmosphere generated by the conference, one hundred students pledged themselves to missionary service, and plans were drawn up for the Student Volunteer Movement for Foreign Missions, which in the next sixty years sent over fourteen thousand men and women abroad as missionaries. With American participation ensured, Wishard now turned his energies toward the rest of the world. There was, he felt, "the necessity of a special movement to enlist the most influential classes in mission lands in the work of evangelization," and it was "to the students in missionary lands . . . [that] we must look for the main body of the missionary army." [29] In 1889 he scraped together enough money to sail for the Orient to recruit that army.

Results in Japan were encouraging, for thriving Associations existed in both Tokyo and Osaka. Harlan Beach, in Japan to help Wishard carry on a summer student conference, spoke glowingly of the Association work in China. Beach was leaving China because of his wife's health, but he and his colleagues felt that the student Association was one of the most important factors in the future of their work.[30] Wishard could pause in China only briefly on his way to India, but in April 1890 he returned, having secured an invitation to speak at the second General Conference of the Protestant Missionaries of China, scheduled for May and, like the one of 1877, to be held in Shanghai. Wishard made his way slowly up the coast, visiting old friends, assessing the possibilities of Association work, and pondering how to plead for missionary support of his dream. By May he was in Shanghai, where again the Protestant missionaries of China had assembled to take stock.[31]

On the surface, China had not changed significantly in thirteen years. Her face was still turned toward the past, and evidences of modernity were limited. But the spirit of the 1890 conference was reasonably confident, for by then the missionary movement was larger and more successful than it had been thirteen years before. There were now 1,296 Western missionaries, male and female, of whom 430 had managed to attend the conference. There were over 37,000 Chinese Protestant Christian communicants. But many of the problems discussed at the 1877 conference were still nagging the missionary movement in 1890. Denominationalism, for example, had increased markedly. Forty-one different denominations were represented in the country, compared with twenty-six in 1877. Even if the hostility of the literary classes seemed to have diminished, and the pejorative term *i* for the western barbarian was rarely heard now, the Chinese upper classes were still not flocking to Christianity. When it was asked if any cases were known of the genuine conversion of a *chü-jen* or "second degree scholar," the replies were "not sufficiently explicit for the record." The hostility of the missionary group itself to the Chinese ethos had scarcely subsided. When W. A. P. Martin issued his plea for toleration of ancestor worship, suggesting that the missionaries leave reform to the influence of divine truth, and when Timothy Richard and Gilbert Reid added that ancestor worship was not entirely idolatrous, they were violently attacked. Furthermore, the question of the quality of Chinese Christians continued to be raised. Although some missionaries defended the graduates who had become Christians at their schools and remained so after entering the business world, John Nevius pointed out that more than a third of the paid agents in Tungchow and Chefoo had been excommunicated.[32]

Many at the conference agreed that the movement urgently needed more missionaries. Wishard's college roommate Robert Mateer, now a missionary in Wei Hsien, appealed on two consecutive days for an influx of ordained men from the United States. The conference formally voted to ask for one thousand ordained ministers over the following five years. Yet many participants clearly realized that a change in approach was also necessary. Typifying the change in attitudes was J. Hudson Taylor, who had once scoffed at Alexander Williamson's defense of education and the press, but was now running a night school. The Reverend M. J. Plumb, a Methodist from

Foochow, suggested establishing industrial and manual training schools. Young J. Allen pleaded for a native Christian university, and John Nevius advanced the need for lecture halls in China.[33] The Society for Diffusion of Christian and General Knowledge, or SDK, was five years old. There thus appeared some recognition at the conference that China was changing, and that missionary work must adapt itself. Perhaps there were other ways to work for the country's salvation. Luther Wishard, carefully appraising his audience, proposed such another method. The time had come, Wishard told his listeners, for special work on the salvation of young men in China. With missionary approval, the Y.M.C.A. would embark on an official program loosely modeled after that in the United States, but shaped to the needs of young Chinese.[34]

Encouraged by favorable remarks from missionaries acquainted with the Association, members of the conference passed a resolution approving Association work in China, but made no practical commitments. To raise support, Wishard began to barnstorm, as was his custom in the United States. He wrote home that between June and October he visited thirty-five missions in fifteen cities, talked to at least a hundred missionaries, and started new student Associations in Shanghai and Peking. In Tungchow he found what he considered to be the best organized student Association in Asia, thriving despite Harlan Beach's departure.[35] Convinced that China was fertile ground for formal Association work by trained secretaries, Wishard sailed for home to get such foreign work underway. "Anywhere, anytime, anything for the Son of God and the sons of Men," he wrote exultantly to his "fellow students" in a letter from Shanghai in May.[36]

Because the American movement in the form of the Association's International Committee was less convinced that it

44

should go anywhere or spend anything outside the country, Wishard had to work desperately to loosen pursestrings and recruit volunteers.[37] Fortunately he had an ally in the new student secretary, John Mott, who lent moral support and vigorously labored for donations from Rockefellers and Fords. Though their money was not yet forthcoming, in the waning days of 1895 David Willard Lyon disembarked from his ship at Shanghai to serve as the first official Y.M.C.A. secretary in China. The son of a missionary, he had been born on a houseboat in Chekiang twenty-five years before, but had gone to the United States to be educated and had stayed there to work in the Y.M.C.A. movement. Now he was back to see what he could do for the young men of China, and he could hardly have picked a more propitious time.

3

THE BEGINNINGS OF SINO-WESTERN COOPERATION

The Chinese Y.M.C.A. made its bow at a favorable moment. Defeat in the Sino-Japanese war had left China stunned, and many Chinese leaders or would-be leaders were turning to Westerners in their midst for guidance. In the capital and the provinces, there were unmistakable signs that the call to reform would now be heeded, and that Westerners could play a role as advisers, teachers, and even organizers of reform. In the treaty ports the clamor was even louder and more effective. The time of widespread Sino-Western cooperation had not yet arrived, but as the Reform Movement in its varied forms throve and languished in the years before the Boxer Uprising, such cooperation as took place provided evidence that the West could play a genuinely helpful role in China's regeneration. The Chinese Y.M.C.A. emerged as one promising agency for collaboration.

In Peking, the traditional fountainhead of reform, Westerners at first hoped to play an important role. As the shock of defeat reverberated throughout the city, men in both official and unofficial circles turned an ear to Western missionaries who for years had been proclaiming the urgent need for reform. Timothy Richard and Gilbert Reid became intimately involved in the birth of the Ch'iang-hsüeh hui or Society for the Study of Self-Strengthening, which initiated the entry into the political sphere of scholars not yet formally in office. Within official circles Reid's influence was also important, for as early as 1896 he succeeded in acquainting numerous officials and literati outside the narrow confines of the Tsungli Yamen or Foreign Office with his ideas on reform. Although

46

the Society for the Study of Self-Strengthening and the subsequent Reform Movement were quickly stifled, they left a legacy of Sino-Western collaboration.

Events in Peking may have promised rapid and widespread solutions by government fiat, but outside of Peking, too, a spirit of inquiry and experiment was emerging. Sometimes it took the shape of debate only, as in the spring of 1896 when the literary chancellor of Shensi Province assigned an essay on the "aims, rules, and advantages" of the Society for the Study of Self-Strengthening, after the society had already been banned.[1] Such discussion caused a stir, though it led to no action. Here and there in the vast mire of Chinese immobility, bubbles of activity were also rising to the surface, as in Hunan, where under the vigorous leadership of Chang Chih-tung, modern schools and industries were developing. In the move toward reform, Westerners played a part whose full extent has not been gauged, though a few examples suggest that their work was varied and imaginative. In Wuchang, missionaries gave science lectures not only at the Western-style college but also at the college of Chinese studies, long considered a stronghold of conservatism.[2] In Tsingchow, the science museum established by Timothy Richard's former colleague, J. S. Whitewright, attracted thousands of students visiting the city for examinations by such curiosities as a steam engine and a stuffed English dray horse.[3] The SDK, whose publications had hitherto enjoyed only a small circulation, found sales soaring. These signs indicated that men were pondering the possible contributions of the West. The most sensitive areas of change, however, continued to be the treaty ports.

The treaty ports, differing from traditional Chinese cities both physically and functionally, had produced a new kind of society. Within each treaty port was a traditional city, with its typical low buildings, dirt roads, dark streets, and enveloping walls. The remainder of the treaty port, however, was given over to the foreign or international area, more Western than Eastern in its tall buildings, macadam roads, and streets lighted by electricity. Sheer physical contrast provided an alternate model for the Chinese vision of what a city might be.

Equally important was the difference in function manifested by the treaty port. As Wolfram Eberhard and Rhoads Murphey have noted, traditional Chinese cities did not exist as political entities but rather as parts of a larger administrative area.[4] Locally based activities were small-scale, organized by blocks or at most by quarters, and usually by special groups such as guilds. Furthermore, since the city's residents were made up of officials and the businessmen who served them, they all depended on the traditional political and social structure rather than being alienated from it. Thus, the traditional Chinese city was a bastion rather than an opponent of the imperial system, and unlike European cities, was not a force for change. In the treaty port, however, the international area presented a different and Western model, for it had administrative unity in the shape of a municipal council, it had city police and fire brigades, and it had a swarm of voluntary associations focusing not only on small groups but also on the community as a whole.

By the end of the nineteenth century, the treaty ports were producing a new kind of Chinese in the form of the modern businessman or comprador. The background, aspirations, habits, and political ideas of the Chinese businessman of 1895 are still somewhat obscure. To the famous scholar and journalist Liang Ch'i-ch'ao, they seemed merely profit-mad moneygrubbers, cravenly imitating Westerners in the hope of personal gain: "They spoke the barbarian language and put on barbarian dress. They emulated the barbarian behavior and followed the barbarian line of arguments . . . But when you asked them whether they had any knowledge of Western natural science, they had none." [5]

However different or less pure their motivations may have been, the treaty port businessmen shared with young intellectuals such as Liang an interest in modernizing society. Their future was linked to a new China, so they had a personal stake in modernization. The treaty ports were still trading cities; in Shanghai, for instance, modern manufacturing did not develop markedly until after 1895. Profit therefore meant the gains realized from dealing with Western import-export firms. Yet the Chinese had learned the ways of Westerners and realized that in a favorable climate they too could become entrepreneurs and manufacturers. Reform and modernization meant money, which was a powerful incentive.

The new student class emerging from modern schools in both the treaty ports and the interior also had a major stake in modernizing society. With a nonclassical education and a background that often barred them from the traditional power structure, these students were linked inexorably to a modern order. Long the outcasts of the old system, Chinese educated in Western knowledge were just beginning to move into prominence as a result of the war. The promotion of several of Yung Wing's boys signaled the promise of a larger role in China for students from modern schools who could successfully straddle the two worlds in which they lived. Although modern students and young businessmen still had low visibility in China in the waning years of the nineteenth century, their presence meant new if subtle challenges to the traditional society. They were not so much an embodiment of modernization as of the yearning toward modernization. And their half-expressed aspirations were soon to become vocal and insistent.

One indication that the treaty ports were swept up in the fever of postwar reform enthusiasm was the vigorous spread of a native press after 1895. In 1894 there were only twelve Chinese newspapers in all of China, but by 1898 there were fifteen in Shanghai alone, as well as a number of periodicals, every one of which advocated a measure of reform.[6] The appearance of so many reform journals in Shanghai indicated that the ports were potential centers of social unrest and social change. In common with the world over, their most restless and experimental members were the young. This became scandalously clear in 1900, when schoolgirls paraded through Shanghai streets wearing boys' clothing, smoking cigarettes, and riding bicycles.[7] In 1896 there were no such sights to titillate the eye and stimulate the pen of shocked ladies from England. But that urban residents did not openly challenge the accepted mores before 1900 did not mean the cities were moribund. As the Y.M.C.A. was quick to discover, the modern young businessmen and students of the treaty ports had needs that an old society could not satisfy, and which an alert new organization might meet.

The partial social dislocation in the growing cities of England and America had provided an opportunity for the Western Y.M.C.A. Large Chinese cities were to prove as receptive. Into the Chinese treaty ports the Association came before any other service group. At first a student Association only, the organization soon expanded to include businessmen. It transmitted a number of skills and values that young Chinese wanted and could utilize. The young Association secretaries were ingratiating, their ideology inoffensive, their services valuable. They did not preach reform; they demonstrated reform.

On a practical day-to-day level, enlisting the Chinese as partners in the work, they laid a road between the not-quite-old and not-yet-new order of society. Compared with the grand plans of Peking, the achievements of this frail new institution may have seemed insignificant, but in four years of work before the Boxer Uprising, the Association earned the reputation among a few influential Chinese of being a trusted partner in reform. After 1900, therefore, Chinese turned in growing numbers to the Y.M.C.A., not merely allowing but urging it to play a greater role in their country's modernization.

It was generally accepted that the stimulus to reform, which meant partial Westernization, must come from Peking, yet as late as 1894 Peking had still been remote and inaccessible to Westerners in all but a physical sense. Although the city of Peking was probably not much smaller or possibly not much larger than Tientsin or Shanghai (perhaps six hundred thousand to one million people, depending on the population guesses accepted), unlike those two treaty ports it remained completely traditional.[8] In 1860 Peking had been forced to accept legations and missionaries, but not trade. Hence, it had no foreign concessions, no Western-style houses, no paved roads, no busy warehouses. Amid the low gray sea of tiles visible from the city wall, only the spire of the French cathedral, considered an eyesore by the Chinese, rose to challenge the height and brilliance of the temples and palaces. The hundred or so Western members of the Customs Inspectorate and the Diplomatic Corps were unable to huddle into a foreign enclave. They lived in Chinese houses, rode on unpaved Chinese streets, choked on Peking dust, and smelled Peking smells. Their life was hardly dull, consisting of French theatricals at the British legation, costume balls at the Russian legation, meets at the foreign race track, and concerts at the residence of Sir Robert Hart, superintendent of the Chinese customs office. They had, however, practically no communication either socially or professionally with the Chinese. The wall surrounding the gentry was solid. Even contacts with the Tsungli Yamen were strictly limited. Such business as came up was transacted mostly by letter or by a rare visit to the yamen, which according to a correspondent for the London *Times,* produced "a fruitless half-hour in a chilly, stone-floored outhouse, sipping green tea with . . . heavily furred ministers, whose dexterity in passing the ball before being collared would have done credit to a Rugby forward." [9] Social contacts were limited to official calls made on new foreign ministers by yamen members, and to an exchange of parties at the Western and Chinese New Year's celebrations. Though the Chinese sometimes warmed up to a remarkable degree under the influence of liquor, they dared not maintain such friendliness for fear of court displeasure. The environment was not conducive to an exchange of ideas.

A potential avenue of information through the missionaries was even more firmly barred. The thirty or so missionaries living in Peking were at the bottom of the social scale assigned to foreigners, as indicated by the price of haircuts, considered an infallible guide: one dollar for a plenipotentiary, thirty cents for an attaché, twenty for a foreign student, and ten for a missionary.[10] Social contact between missionaries and the Chinese upper classes was almost unknown. In 1892 Gilbert Reid declared that he knew of only three or four missionaries anywhere in the country who had ever met a mandarin socially.[11] Missionaries were not even allowed access to Chinese officials unless they came on formal business and were accompanied by foreign officials. Thus, it was not strange that the power groups in Peking remained almost totally sealed from foreign contact and knowledge.

In 1895, however, cracks appeared in the wall of Peking's aloofness. Reid had spent a period of time on furlough in the United States, during which he occupied himself in pleading publicly for better legislation to protect Chinese laborers. When he returned to Peking in the autumn of 1894, his work had become known to Chinese officials, which paved the way for better relations. Reid's arrival coincided with a changeover in power and attitude in Peking, as the government began to realize that China was losing the war. This time the American's vigorous advances and talk of reform met a friendlier response among court officials than he had elicited during the days when he was living in a Chinese temple and making unsuccessful attempts to meet the upper classes.[12]

Although the new cordiality of Peking officials was gratifying, Reid realized that these men were unable to breach the wall of conservatism in the city. The real hope for reform lay with young men not in office, who were less timid. When Reid first met the scholar-reformer K'ang Yu-wei is uncertain, but soon after Timothy Richard arrived in Peking in September 1895, Reid arranged a meeting between the two, which took place on October 17. That the spirit of reform was strong among such men, Reid was convinced. He wrote two years later: "An English missionary, the Rev. Timothy Richard, was visiting Peking, whom I introduced to several of the more active leaders in the new movement. We had several conferences together, until what was known as a 'Reform Club' [the Ch'iang Hsüeh-hui] was actually started by these young men in this conservative centre of the Empire. Their spirit of reform was . . . more literary and educational than moral. They lacked the strong underlying principles of an active morality, made living by religious convictions. Nevertheless the movement was encouraging. A beginning was made." [13]

When the society was abolished by the government in January 1896 and its effectiveness temporarily eliminated, Reid's brief hope that the young could reform China disappeared. The progress in Sino-Western cooperation, however, had been real, and upon this achievement he sought to build a new edifice. He turned his attention to the officials and older literati with whom he had achieved such an unprecedented social and intellectual success. He conceived the idea of founding an institute, in cooperation with interested Chinese and Western individuals, that would serve as a social meeting place for both Chinese and Westerners, and which would disseminate secular, modern knowledge to the upper classes. Backed by representatives of several countries, he set to work trying to raise the money and to obtain Chinese sanction for the project, which he termed the International Institute.[14]

It was into this hope-filled environment that the new Y.M.C.A. secretary entered. Willard Lyon, the new secretary from the United States, arrived in Shanghai at the time when the Society for the Study of Self-Strengthening was being formed and Reid was enlarging his acquaintance with Peking officials. The Western community experienced a sense of optimism about the possibilities of reform in China and the potential for a partnership between Chinese and Westerners. To Lyon, the awakening of the young scholars was particularly exciting. The opportunities in Peking for a youth worker from the West appeared great, especially since as far back as 1890, Peking missionaries had asked for an official Y.M.C.A. representative to work with the traditional students who came to the city for examinations.[15] Lyon, however, did not know

Mandarin and realized that he would cut a sorry figure in Peking intellectual circles. He turned his back regretfully on the capital, hoping to make it his headquarters sometime in the near future, and began to assess his possible usefulness in the treaty ports.[16]

Missionaries in the treaty ports were aware that they had not been able to devote sufficient attention to the needs of young men. On February 1, 1891, for instance, the Shanghai missionary body had sent to the United States a request for an Association man to work with three types of youths: Chinese who had not learned English, English-speaking Chinese (who were Westernized merely to the extent that they had "added the list of European vices to their own"), and foreigners.[17] On June 17, 1894, Chefoo missionaries called for the establishment of an Association that could carry on work similar to that of the city Associations in the United States and Great Britain.[18] These calls, however, concerned young businessmen. Lyon, who sprang from the American student movement, felt that his first obligation was to the Chinese student. Thus, neither the Shanghai nor the Chefoo requests were met, for an invitation from Tientsin seemed more promising and urgent.

In 1895 Tientsin was a city of something under a million people, divided into the walled Chinese city and the bustling International Settlement that sprawled along the winding Pei River. Ninety-two and a half miles by water or eighty by road from Peking, sixty-five miles by road from Taku, the city's situation at the confluence of several rivers and large canals made it both the marketing center for the trade of the northern provinces (Chihli, Shansi, Shensi, Kansu, and North Honan) and the stopping place for visitors on the way to Peking. By comparison with Shanghai, its foreign trade was small—in 1890, 3.0 percent of the total, compared with

Shanghai's 45.9 percent—but its prospects seemed excellent. Administratively the city had grown steadily in importance, for so many important visitors passed through on their way to or from royal audiences that in 1860 the Chihli viceroy had moved his official yamen there from Paotingfu.[19]

Tientsin was, in addition, Li Hung-chang's model city, with a railroad, a telegraph line, a vigorous press, and six modern schools. The new Tientsin university, known as the Chung-hsi Hsüeh-t'ang or Sino-Western College, had recently opened in quarters below the British concession on Taku Road. The city supported a prosperous Chinese business community. Missionaries wrote that Tientsin was much more open than Peking to the forces that made for civilization and Christianity.[20]

For Lyon, the deciding factor was the peculiar nature of the student body in the modern government schools. Tientsin was the center of progressive education in China. As Knight Biggerstaff has pointed out, an almost indispensable prerequisite to attending the modern schools was a knowledge of English, because modern information was not yet available either in written Chinese or from Chinese instructors.[21] Thus, most of the students in these schools knew "more or less" English, according to resident missionaries.[22] Since many were not from Mandarin-speaking areas, they were often actually dependent on English for communication with one another.[23] To a Westerner who had not yet learned Chinese, such a linguistically trained group presented an excellent opportunity for temporary service.

The students, moreover, were already partly acquainted with Western ideas. Most of them had learned their English in mission schools. Lyon discovered that the mission schools were the principal feeders into all six Tientsin colleges, that most of the students had some exposure to the missionary version of modern Western society, and that at least ten percent were professed Christians.[24] All these factors promised a fertile soil in which to plant the Y.M.C.A. of China.

On December 8, 1895, the first official student Y.M.C.A. in China under the leadership of a trained secretary was opened in Tientsin. It started in a friendly atmosphere. Local missionaries and teachers rounded up about a hundred students for the organizational meeting, and sixty-four decided to become members.[25] The press hailed the Association's arrival. A devout lady from Cleveland, Ohio, Mrs. Livingstone Taylor, had tentatively promised ten thousand dollars for a student center. Buoyed by the interest in Tientsin and by the promise of support from the United States, Lyon installed himself in rented quarters and cast about for a program that might link the Association to the aspirations and needs of the modern urban students. A number of factors, some deliberate and some chance, were on his side.

The first asset was Lyon himself. To the young Chinese of Tientsin, Lyon and the men who later joined him were like a breath of fresh air. They were well educated, but not scholarly academics like many of the missionaries. They were concerned with moral and spiritual values, but they were not theologians, even though several of the early arrivals were ordained ministers. They were practical businessmen, but not interested in profit for itself. They were pragmatists rather than theoreticians. Their type is familiar in the United States: optimistic, versatile, motivated by a sense of obligation to serve. In our time their spiritual descendants often become members of the Peace Corps, and then, as now, their personal qualities appealed to other young people.

Moreover, the Association happily brought to China no constricting set of rules. As China was unknown territory, Lyon and his colleagues were wisely burdened by few regulations. Their philosophy was that of the American Association: to serve all young men in their multiple needs, and to persuade them to serve others. Precisely how the Chinese Association would do so was left in large measure to the ingenuity of the new secretaries. This flexibility proved a major asset.[26]

Along with the permissiveness, however, went a few rules that generally proved a sensible compromise between the demands of the American parent Association and the possibilities inherent in China. Basically, the Association in America stipulated that the Chinese Association, like all others started by the International Committee outside the United States, should become self-propagating, self-governing, and self-supporting as quickly as possible. Lyon was, in other words, pledged to start not a movement that would be an alien growth, but one that would become truly indigenous. This plan reflected the earnest belief that the Chinese should have a part in shaping their own destiny, and the leadership in developing their own institutions. It was perhaps the happiest decision of all.

Implicit in the idea of indigenization was the idea of self-support. The American Association realized that it, or individuals sympathetic to its aims, would have to help Associations abroad in certain ways. The Chinese were not expected to pay the salaries of American secretaries who went to China, nor to pledge money for buildings. In Lyon's case both salary and building came not from Association funds but from one individual, Mrs. Taylor, and in the early days secretaries who wanted to go to China actually had to find their own patrons.[27] Yet the American ethos of the time dictated that ventures should prove their worth by finding local backing. This financial dictum covered Associations both in the United States and

58

abroad. Before any buildings donated by American philanthropists could be erected, Chinese in the city under consideration had to provide the entire cost of the building lot. Running expenses had to be met locally. If the Chinese wanted an Association, in other words, they must support it; if not, the Association would be built on sand and would not deserve to survive.[28] This ruling tended to hamper Association growth in some directions, but it did not prove an impediment for several years, and it probably achieved the aim of financial stability.

The Association's religious stand could not, it was obvious, please everyone. On the one hand, the *North China Herald's* expressed hope that the organization would be totally secular was impossible.[29] The Association was clearly Christian, and its program would inevitably include some Bible work. Lyon himself was an ordained minister, as were several of the early secretaries. The very roots of the movement lay in devotional Christianity. Furthermore, many potential financial backers in the United States were orthodox evangelical Christians. Given all of these factors, the American parent committee had stipulated that boards of directors and the category of members known as "active" or voting be uniformly members of the evangelical churches.[30] However, a wide latitude was permitted in defining a Christian Association's attitudes and duties. Association secretaries in fact tended toward the liberal position in Christianity, which substituted cheer and good works for guilt and strident proselytizing. They were eager to eschew religious formalism in their work. They thus deemphasized orthodoxy from the start. Such religious work as was carried on reflected the same disavowal of dogma that had characterized Dwight Moody's work in the United States.

Furthermore, Christianity might be the ground from which

sprang the Y.M.C.A.'s vitality, but proselytism was not the Association's sole or even major aim. The spirit of the Chinese Association, no matter what letters were sent home to prospective backers, was one of service, not conversion. The secretaries were called *kan shih*, meaning secretary or manager, a term with no religious connotation. Most of the program was secular. Thus, when the Association declared that membership was open to all young men regardless of religious or agnostic convictions, it enabled non-Christians to join without a constant sense of pressure. Years later one of the Association secretaries remarked that the churches in China said in essence, "Join us and then we'll be your friends," whereas the Association said simply, "Come and be our friend." [31] Chinese could partake in the religious program or not. It soon became evident that many young Chinese in Tientsin who avowed that they would never become Christian were nevertheless associating themselves enthusiastically with the Y.M.C.A. Without their support, the organization could not have flourished as it did.

The brevity of the rules meant that there were few curbs upon the imagination, and that a versatile program might be developed. As far as Lyon could tell, there were no general service organizations in Tientsin for students or, as he termed it, "for student uplifting." [32] After investigation, he issued a pamphlet designed to whet the appetites of prospective members. The pamphlet described the Association as: "a band of earnest young men, united for their own improvement along physical, social, mental and spiritual lines, and for the purpose of helping other young men along similar lines . . . It holds meetings for debates, for listening to lectures, for social enjoyment, for music, for Bible study, and for prayer and conference." Mrs. Taylor, Lyon's sponsor, had gone to China,

60

visited the Great Wall, surveyed the state of spiritual life in Tientsin, and presented ten thousand dollars for the first Y.M.C.A. building in China. The pamphlet announced that the new building would have a reading room, a lecture hall, parlor, library, educational rooms, gymnasium, baths, and a game room. Any young man of good moral character who spoke some English was invited to join.[33]

The announcement of this ambitious program was well timed. The Y.M.C.A. had appeared, wrote its Chinese national secretary David Yui in a memoir of the 1920's, at just the right moment. Young Chinese were tired of words and theories. They were anxious to learn the secrets of the West and to practice reform. The new Association promised both theory and practice, with a varied program that was sensitive to Chinese needs.[34] First under Lyon, then after 1898 under the leadership of Robert Gailey, the Tientsin Association worked to fulfill the promises made in its membership pamphlet. The bulk of the work that any one man and a handful of assistants could do was small, and their records are scarce. Yet it is clear that much of the significant work carried on later by the Association, when it had millions of dollars and hundreds of secretaries, and many of the attitudes engendered by it among the Chinese, appeared in microcosm in those early days.

One key to attracting young students was an educational program that would partly satisfy their clamor for information about the modern world. A knowledge of English was invaluable to an aspiring student or businessman. So great was the desire to learn English, wrote the Tientsin correspondent of the *North China Herald* early in 1897, that throughout the city, men who barely knew the language were setting themselves up as English teachers and finding prospective students.[35] The students in modern schools, whom Lyon had discovered knew "more or less English," were anxious to improve their skills. Into this partial vacuum Lyon was able to move easily, being well equipped by his background and education to teach English. He devised a program of language instruction that set the pattern for an important part of Y.M.C.A. educational work for years to come. It was evidently the first such program presented under nonmissionary auspices, for he wrote home that, "in point of time the Association was the first, and in point of influence the leading center of western education under nonmissionary control." [36]

The decision to teach English as a starting point of contact illustrated the Association's pragmatic approach. The Association did not care whether its courses led to the counting house instead of the church. Many missionaries had resented being used as a means to an end, whereas the Association intended to be used as a means. If English was what the students wanted, they should have it. By the end of 1897 the newly constituted board of directors planned also to offer courses in arithmetic, with special evening lectures in history, science, and other unspecified subjects for sufficiently fluent students. The Association even hoped that the courses would constitute formal preparation for the Tientsin university.[37] So varied was the work of missionary boards in the decades preceding the Association's arrival that it is impossible to declare whether part-time instruction of this sort had been an aspect of church work in Tientsin, although part-time instruction was not new to China. It was the Association, however, that became noted for offering practical instruction at convenient hours, a concept that later had widespread repercussions in the country. The modest program in Tientsin was the beginning.

Since education had always meant to the Y.M.C.A. a greater range of activities than formal class work alone, Lyon also pursued this wider aim. Dr. B. C. Atterbury, once a member of the New York Y.M.C.A. and now a teacher at the Tientsin medical school (the I-hsüeh t'ang), had started a "Mutual Improvement Club" among English-speaking students there. Lyon took over the club, renamed it the Literary Club of the Y.M.C.A., and initiated a series of lectures whose subjects have unfortunately not been recorded.[38] He was thus doing what Timothy Richard had long advocated, what missionaries were beginning to do here and there in the country, and what Reid was hoping to effect through the International Institute.

There were apparently no public reading rooms in Tientsin, although there had been reading rooms for Chinese in Amoy, Chefoo, and fitfully at the Shanghai Polytechnic Institute.[39] In its reading room, the Association supplied a number of periodicals in English for members. The first publications were mainly religious, but by 1898 the reading room subscribed to *Harper's Weekly,* the New York *Evening Post, Century,* and a number of other secular publications.[40] The wide range of reading material available in the room proved a drawing card. Lyon even tried to encourage a sense of cohesiveness among the members by starting a student bulletin, which in the first years saw sporadic publication. In 1896 the bulletin was issued in English as a semiannual publication, called *China's Young Men,* and shortly thereafter became a monthly.[41] By 1897 it was retitled the *Hsüeh-hsiao pao* or *Chinese Intercollegian,* to reflect the fact that a national organization of sorts had been formed incorporating the Tientsin Association and mission school student Y.M.C.A.'s. The bulletin included two pages in English and four in Chinese. Distribution reached 700 copies a month, whereupon the volume of work forced Lyon to discontinue publication.[42] In 1899 Robert Gailey, the second Y.M.C.A. secretary to arrive, revived the bulletin as a regular monthly and gradually devoted more and more space to general and Association news.[43] In an effort to achieve the proper tone for the young, the publication later experimented with expanded content and new stylistic devices.

The educational phase of its program loomed largest in the early days, but from the start the Association made an attempt to pursue its quadruple aim. The Chinese Association sought to serve the whole man in four ways: through *chih* or knowledge, *t'i* or physical work, *te* or spiritual work, and *ch'ün* or the sense of community.[44] Then and later, the contributions made by secretaries outside as well as within the intellectual sphere tangibly demonstrated their dedication to the total aim. In the area of physical work, for example, Lyon found that his best entry to the Chinese was through their new interest in military fitness. The Tientsin university had inaugurated a course in military drill. Lyon, a gentle and scholarly man, went there once a week to teach the course. While his ability to teach this subject was not surprising, since most American schools provided such training at the time, his willingness to do so indicated his pragmatic response to the Chinese needs.[45] The ability to reach out to the Chinese was characteristic of the more competent secretaries. Later, Robert Gailey studied Chinese theater and became a devotee of Chinese cooking; Eugene Barnett studied Buddhism; and Amos Hoagland went into the streets to learn to know the coolies. These men refused to stay aloof from their environment.

In the religious area designated by the word *te*, Lyon patterned his work after earlier student association attempts in China and the United States. Dr. Atterbury of the Tientsin medical school had previously formed a weekly prayer meeting for medical school students, which Lyon took over and tried to reshape around the concept of student control and participa-

64

tion. He was attempting to introduce to students what Harlan Beach called "the luxury of doing good." He had earlier encouraged students to help raise money for the new building site, and his modest success in this venture encouraged him.[46] Inasmuch as association philosophy maintained that the students needed a sense of community responsibility, the Association persistently wondered how to give them this sense. Not for a few more years did the secretaries develop a major program for encouraging and harnessing the latent dynamism of Chinese students, but in these early years the germ was already there.

If one were to dig assiduously in missionary records, it might be possible to find a precedent for everything the new Association was doing. Other men had given English lessons. Others had enjoyed their Chinese acquaintances and invited them to dinner, studied Buddhism or art. Many had contributed to the sum of experience upon which later men such as the Association secretaries could draw. Timothy Richard and Calvin Mateer had learned from Matthew Ricci; Willard Lyon and his associates learned by example, reputation, and consultation from Richard and Mateer. Receptivity to other ideas was part of the Association's genius. Yet there was something new about the enterprise, too: its scope, versatility, pragmatism, and perhaps most of all its intangible, unmeasurable quality of youth and affability. When in the 1920's the Chinese looked back from the perspective of several years, they noted how versatile and adaptable the Association had been and still was. Perhaps the growing nationalism of the 1920's made them place even more emphasis on one factor than it had received in 1896, although it unquestionably was important then also. This factor was the Association's insistence upon becoming Chinese.[47] Much more quickly than any church-

backed organization in China, the Y.M.C.A. set out to involve
the Chinese in leadership. Locally, nationally, and internation-
ally, there was to be no doubt that the Chinese Y.M.C.A. was
trying to become indigenous. This thread ran through both the
newly developing national organization and the Association's
international connections.

Although the Tientsin Association was the only one organized and guided under official Y.M.C.A. auspices, it was not
the only student Y.M.C.A. in China. Mission school student
associations, organized by principals or teachers, had come
and gone, victims of vagrant enthusiasm, feeble organization,
and lack of leadership. Up to early 1896 only four of these
seem to have survived.[48] In the fall of that year, Lyon undertook a whirlwind tour of the country with John Mott of the
Y.M.C.A.'s International Committee, a man blessed with a
genius for organization, unlimited energy, massive good looks,
and a staggering capacity for raising money. Mott had become
not only college secretary of the International Committee but
also secretary of a new organization called the World Student
Christian Federation, formed with Y.M.C.A. encouragement in
1895 to knit students of the world together. Under Mott's
energetic leadership, twenty-two mission school student Associations were formed in China in the autumn months of 1896,
making a total of twenty-seven such Associations in China.[49]
In November 1896, the Y.M.C.A. held a national convention in
Shanghai, just a year after Lyon had set foot in the country. It
was the way Mott did things. The student Associations were
grouped into an organization formally designated as the Yu-t'u
hui or College Young Men's Christian Association of China, a
National Committee was formed, and the Association made
clear its intention to become a Chinese movement.[50] Half the
members of the National Committee, it was stipulated, must

be Chinese.[51] This percentage far outstripped the Chinese representation in any of the formal church groups. Actually, Chinese representation on the committee soon went well beyond 50 percent.[52] Convention officers were also to be Chinese. At the first convention, most of the leading figures were Westerners—seventeen mission school presidents, for example, were present.[53] But by 1899, at the second national convention, all officers were Chinese except for two: Devello Sheffield, the chairman, and Henry Luce, father of the publisher.[54] This policy was good psychology in years when China's sense of pride was suffering continual setbacks.

Locally, too, the Association demonstrated its intention of being a cooperative Sino-Western venture. In Tientsin, Chinese quickly appeared on the board of directors: most of them Christian educators, but one, Wong Kok-shan, a businessman who later became prominent in the iron and steel mills of Wuhan.[55] As early as 1899 Lyon urged that the Association establish and subsidize from America a training school for Chinese secretaries.[56] When the first city Association opened in Shanghai in 1900, it had on its roster a full-time Chinese secretary, S. K. Tsao.[57] Eventually the number of Chinese secretaries far outstripped the number of Westerners.

On the international scene, John Mott made it clear that the Chinese should hold positions of dignity by requesting their active participation in conventions of the World Student Christian Federation, to which the Y.M.C.A. expected to send delegates. M. U. Ting went as a delegate to a student meeting in Northfield, Massachusetts, and a Professor Huang from Nanking University went to a world convention in Paris in 1900.[58] Such attempts at indigenization did not, however, win widespread publicity, as the Association was a tiny institution engaged in minuscule operations. But the sincere attempt to indigenize the movement elicited a favorable Chinese response wherever it became known and was enormously important in shaping the future.

By early 1897 there was no question that the little Tientsin Association was well liked and useful. Both the expansionist urge and conditions in China itself seemed to dictate the spread of the work to other cities. To begin with, the climate of reform seemed to have brightened in the country. After a period of discouragement, Gilbert Reid had succeeded in obtaining official sanction for his International Institute from the Tsungli Yamen in March 1897. This was the first time a foreign program under foreign auspices had been sanctioned by the Chinese government. Armed with ambitious plans for a public auditorium, small classrooms, a science museum, library, and reception rooms, Reid had already secured the backing of Westerners in the Shanghai business community and had departed for the United States in hopes of raising more money. An interesting aspect of the Tsungli Yamen's decision was that it had consistently refused cooperation until Reid's father died and Reid announced he was giving up his attempts in order to go home for the mourning period. This evidence of filial piety, he was astonished to find, elicited yamen support promptly.[59] Reid's unprecedented success seemed to signal a new era of good feelings in China. The official classes were willing to meet foreigners as never before, reported W. A. P. Martin to the North China Tract Society in May.[60] Even the most conservative officials favored schools for teaching the Western sciences in every province. Such news generated additional optimism among Westerners.

The news of Reid's success quickened Lyon's already urgent calls for reinforcements. What Reid was planning to do with older Chinese, Lyon wanted to do with traditional students.

68

The Association, in fact, felt that Reid was using an Association program stripped of its Christian elements.[61] Reid's progress convinced the Association that the time for expansion was at hand. It was not that Lyon felt he was wasting his energies in Tientsin. On the contrary, he had pointed out on several occasions that Tientsin students would hold a unique place in controlling the affairs of the new China "which is soon to be." [62] But then and later the Y.M.C.A. was tugged in two directions: toward the modern sectors of China with which it had a natural affinity, and toward the traditional sector, which often seemed to hold the real power and with which it had fewer natural bonds. Although Lyon genuinely believed in the eventual leadership of the modern students, he realized that for the foreseeable future power lay with the traditional students. Toward all of them he felt a deep sense of obligation that led him to desire immediate expansion for the Association movement: "I want to urge that America is peculiarly responsible for China, and therefore America's young men for China's young men," he wrote to Richard Morse of the International Committee. "America has excluded the Chinaman from her own borders, and therefore Christian America owes it all the more to exemplify to China the true love that exists in the Christlike hearts." [63] This need to make recompense for the American immigration policy, the need for a secretary-at-large to start new Associations, and an understandable sense of being overworked, all impelled Lyon to ask for help.

Fortunately for the fledgling movement, John Mott had been infected with enthusiasm for China during his visit. He was also struck by the power of the ruling class. The literati-officials, he wrote, were the Gibraltar of the East, but the students might be the lever that could move them.[64] With Mott's backing, moral and organizational rather than financial, reinforcements arrived in 1898 in the shape of Robert Gailey, Robert Lewis, and Fletcher Brockman. After an initial period, Gailey became secretary of the Tientsin Association, Lewis went to Shanghai to experiment with young businessmen, and Brockman became the national secretary. Lyon himself began to concentrate on student work.

By the time that the new men arrived, the bubble of enthusiasm in Peking had exploded. The Hundred Days of Reform had come and gone, the emperor was locked away, and the conservatives were back in power. Yet as the secretaries traveled around the country, talking to friends and assessing the environment, they became convinced that reform had been postponed, not stopped. There were unmistakable signs that Western education would be encouraged. If they were not entering so hospitable a country as they had hoped, neither were they entering one deaf to their message.[65]

In Tientsin, Robert Gailey continued Lyon's work. A Princeton Theological Seminary graduate of superior intelligence, he added to his own good training a keen interest in China. Gailey had been an all-American halfback at Princeton, known to his contemporaries as "Center-Rush Gailey." A robust, outgoing man, he radiated an intense love of life that commended itself to the Chinese taste. His capacity for eating was legendary; later in life it took an oversized rickshaw and a double complement of men to move him around. These heroic qualities were not yet evident, but from the start Gailey was liked by the Chinese. As he continued Lyon's educational program, enlarged the reading room, promoted an interest in playing football among the students, and labored to learn the Chinese language, he developed a good reputation in the city. Tientsin businessmen urged him to start a program for young

70

clerks, and he began to ponder how to reach the still unapproachable gentry.

In Shanghai, Robert Lewis found a considerable number of young businessmen interested in becoming part of a city Association. The sizable missionary and business community was behind him.[66] Early in 1900, he organized a group of one hundred and fifty charter members among the young comprador class, most of them, he reported, being college graduates.[67] This was the first formal city Association in China. Like the Tientsin Association, Shanghai offered evening language classes. Lewis filled out the program by a bicycle club, a tennis club, and religious work. Nestled within the International Concession, the new Shanghai Association promised to serve many useful purposes.

By the early days of 1900, there were thus clear indications of the areas where the Chinese Y.M.C.A. could expect cooperation and welcome. The mission schools presented no problem; school presidents merely authorized a student Association and generally left it to its own devices. The possibilities of city organizations serving young businessmen seemed excellent, if Shanghai was a guide. Modern students could be approached through English classes at least. It was not a bad record for a handful of years.

But to a few thoughtful and experienced Westerners, the Y.M.C.A. seemed to offer a brilliant approach to the traditional classes of China as well. Fletcher Brockman, a man of distinct intelligence and initiative, bustled about China visiting Associations, asking for advice, and looking for avenues of future progress. Both Calvin Mateer and Timothy Richard urged him to develop an Association program for traditional students and literati. Both agreed to speak at the second national convention, held in 1899, and they advised the Association to devote itself to the task of winning over the upper classes in which endeavor they had long been involved themselves.[68]

The Association could not devote all of its resources to this aim, because obligations to students and young businessmen came first. Work with the literati was added, however, to the list of objectives. As the century approached its end, that list was growing swiftly. The challenges in China were great. At best, the young organization could plan in the immediate future only a modest and steady expansion of facilities, so as to include businessmen and enlarge educational services. Other cities might develop Associations if money became available.

Then abruptly the situation changed with the Boxer Uprising. Tientsin was overrun, sacked, and burned. The modern schools lay in ruins. The little Y.M.C.A. building was wrecked. Soldiers of a dozen nations paraded through a city where not only buildings but also a variety of illusions and dreams had gone up in smoke. It was a bitter development for the Americans, bitter for the moderate Chinese, and bitterest of all, perhaps, for the arch conservatives who had gambled on the old order, lost, and been stripped of their fantasies about Chinese power. In Tientsin, as elsewhere in China, the Chinese appraised their position and the possible courses of action. Where could they turn? Whom could they trust? Few Western groups could qualify, but one acceptable group, it immediately became apparent, was the new Y.M.C.A. Somewhat to its astonishment, the Association thus found itself playing a far larger role in China's modernization than it had expected.

4

ALLIANCE AND CHANGE, 1900–1911

In the decade following the Boxer Uprising, China at last attempted to set itself to the task of reform. Prodded by a mounting clamor of political criticism, the government tried to modernize the economic system, renovate the law codes, improve transportation, and develop an adequate educational system. The major landmarks of social change were the end of the examination system, the proliferation of new schools, the flow of students abroad, and the growth of an active urban middle class. Although political progress in the last years of the Ch'ing era was limited, social change was continuous. Because of the imperial government's resistance to political innovation, however, it has been common to underrate social and economic progress during the Ch'ing era. Yet national and local governments set in motion many changes, and paralleling or sometimes deriving from these government moves were many private measures that altered urban life. Anecdote and detail are more available than statistics to convey a picture of the newly bustling cities experimenting with fads and fashions, questioning ancient traditions, appraising new ideas, and occasionally taking new steps. They show that many of the cities of China changed markedly between 1900 and 1911.

Some modernization recorded by the tourists, diplomats, and businessmen visiting the country was only superficial. Peking's main street was macadamized, and the sidewalks were paved, but sewers were nonexistent. In Chengtu, lights were installed on sedan chairs, though these vehicles continued to be hauled by human beings. Some novelties, like the temporary rage for lead pencils in Szechwan, proved passing fancies.[1] Yet the major physical changes in Tientsin and

Shanghai were impressive, as walls went down, tree-lined boulevards appeared, and electric tramways and tall buildings replaced the rubble. Moreover, accompanying the physical changes were real and irreversible modifications in society. Girls' schools were founded; merchants turned to political action. The once-docile students began to mass in the streets, march, and strike.

One could almost chart the temper of the young by the fate of the queue, that symbol of Chinese subservience to Manchu rule. In 1900, when the scholar Chang Ping-lin cut off his queue before a public meeting, the gesture was revolutionary and dangerous.[2] Ten years later, queue-cutting demonstrations were a gala feature of Shanghai political life, and for many young people the gesture was no longer political but merely a normal social adaptation to practical needs.[3] In an athletic meet held as part of the Nanking Industrial Exposition of 1910, for instance, a pole-vaulter lost his final jump because his flying queue misplaced the bar, and that night he simply chopped it off.[4] Thus far had China moved in ten years.

A complex interweaving of content and process underly social change, and no one has yet compiled an exhaustive list of the preconditions for such reform. These factors, though, seem necessary: desire, a real or envisioned model, initiators, and a process; or to express it more succinctly, a why, what, who, and how of change. Reform in China was as formal as the imperial government's decision to establish a public school system modeled after that of Japan, or as informal as the decision of the young athlete to chop off his queue. Yet in both cases desire was coupled with a concept and a process. The individual or group who could contribute to this complex pattern would influence the direction of reform.

By 1900, there was little question that a large number of

urban Chinese desired reform. Testimony pours from American letters of the era: "The floodgates are open." [5] "Tientsin is in a rage for Western externals." [6] "I find no one who admits to being a conservative." "Not to be a reformer is to be politically dead." [7] "The people will not wait; we cannot go slowly if we would." [8] Such themes echo and re-echo in the following years. Between concept and consummation, however, lay an abyss. The general model of gradual reform, patterned after Japan, was at first unquestioned, for the Chinese in power wanted only a comfortable if energetic change, not an overturning of society. Yet general enthusiasm was not enough. Technical problems arose. such as learning how to start a school, do double-entry bookkeeping, or control tuberculosis. It was because the Chinese modernizers could not at first cope with these specific problems that foreigners, even Westerners, became necessary partners.

It is generally conceded that Westerners played a far smaller role in the Ch'ing reform era than they had hoped. Since the place of Western businessmen as transmitters of change has not been assessed, further research may indicate that they figured significantly as informal teachers of modern ways. The more formal transmission of new ideas, however, was relegated to educators, many of whom were missionaries. Although the missionaries were educating about sixty thousand students a year by this time, they had long awaited appearance of a Chinese desire for reform, which they hoped would permit them to move into government schools where they might influence far larger numbers. Most, however, were soon disappointed. China's pressing need did not mean an uncritical acceptance of foreign ideas or skills, for entangled with the desire to emulate foreign models was the old struggle to maintain Chinese values. The meaning of the Chinese *t'i* or "essence" is as debatable as the Japanese *kokutai* or the "American way of life," but elusiveness of definition does not mean nonexistence. To some, the essence of China was its moral basis; to others, the preservation of a family system; to still others a nascent Chinese nationalism—but to all Chinese that essence dictated a critical scrutiny of foreign models and foreign helpers. This meant that few Western missionaries could participate in the mainstream of the reform movement, because their insistence on preaching Christianity offended Chinese values; Japanese teachers were used instead. It also meant that the Chinese adapted foreign institutions and took over leadership themselves with all possible speed. The result was not that foreigners were prevented from participating in the process of reform, but that they were allowed to do so only if they could accept Chinese values, not threaten them.

Over and beyond the problems of models and values, there remained the equally pressing questions of leadership and organization of reform. Above the primary level of personal adaptation, leaders must be found to introduce social change to the many other levels and groups in Chinese society, and means must be determined by which these leaders could gain acceptance for their innovations. In 1900 these were not easy problems to solve.

The natural leaders of the country were government officials, many of whom by 1900 had been mildly or strongly infected by the virus of reform and had made attempts to introduce change. Gilbert Reid remarked upon the diffusion of reform-minded officials into many provinces after about 1895.[9] About 1901 a traveler in Szechwan found an alert and modern-minded upper official group, among whom were a brother of one of Yung Wing's boys and a graduate of the Foochow Arsenal.[10] Yung Wing men, rescued from the obscurity they had suffered since their return from American schools, were themselves moving toward high office. Notable among them were T'ang Shao-yi, a taotai in Tientsin attached to the customs board, and Liang Tun-yen, who became minister of foreign affairs for the imperial government in 1908. At the uppermost level, traditionally trained men such as Chang Chih-tung and Yuan Shih-k'ai possessed enough power to initiate considerable change. But top officials alone were not enough. As the reformers connected with the ill-fated Hundred Days had discovered, stolidity or resistance at lower bureaucratic levels was massive and could be fatal. With the central government growing increasingly impotent, officials needed more than ever the collaboration of their old allies, the gentry.

China's gentry had provided leadership at both village and town levels. "The social, educational and official systems of China have tended to give the educated classes control of the destinies of the nation," wrote Li Hung-chang to Gilbert Reid in 1897. "Whether such a monopoly of power be good or bad need not now be considered; it exists, and the practical question is how to turn it into beneficent and useful channels." [11] The power of the upper classes, reported Fletcher Brockman, was beyond belief.[12] Yet now that China was turning toward reform, the gentry were rendered powerless by their ignorance, resulting from a longtime refusal to study or to countenance change. Until they could educate themselves to the needs of a modern society, they could not lead China.

Merchants and students, the newly emerging elites, were better acquainted with the requirements for reform. More than the established elites, certainly, the modern merchant class was pressing for change. In 1902 the government officially recognized its importance to China by organizing *shang-hui*, modern Chambers of Commerce. As the Ch'ing reform era wore on, these shang-hui supplanted the old guilds in economic power. They also showed themselves capable of asserting political power and proved amenable to social change.[13] In a sense, as the very embodiment of change, merchants were entitled to become the leaders in modernization. Yet accustomed to their low social status and to the depredations of the official world, their new-found importance at first sat uneasily upon them. They sometimes preferred to work under protective cover while learning the leadership role. As for the other emerging elite, the students, they did not actually constitute an elite during most of the reform era, for they were still seeking to define their role, both politically and socially. They, above all, needed direction.

Into this partial and temporary leadership vacuum in China, determined individuals or small groups with knowledge, a sense of organization, and persistence were able to move, providing they could find a sympathetic audience. An official with the power to generate activity among the bureaucracy, a member of the gentry with enough energy to found and staff a modern school, or a Westerner who could introduce an alien institution without offending the Chinese were all able to make a genuine contribution. The times flung up new opportunities and new leaders. Thus, the small and little-known Chinese Y.M.C.A. achieved during the years from 1900 to 1911 a scope and reputation disproportionate to its size and even to its original objectives. Until 1905 the Association was limited to the cities of Shanghai and Tientsin, but by 1907 at least eight cities on the mainland had branches of some sort, and thereafter the work spread rapidly. Membership and support kept pace among the Chinese.

Its growth was explained by the fact that the Association stood for gradualist Western change. Its values paralleled those of traditional China, yet contained a dynamic that appealed to modernizers. As the first example of a modern youth institution in an age when the young were at last receiving attention, it carried on useful services that were reforms in themselves: vocational education, athletics, recreation, professional science lectures. In many areas it took over temporary leadership or helped the floundering Chinese leaders, as in starting schools, planning opium-control campaigns, providing famine relief, assisting students overseas, and organizing youth activities. The cooperation of the Association with various Chinese interest groups made the work possible, and the success of its work in turn made further alliances possible. Partly by natural evolution and partly by design, therefore, the Association found that it had acquired firm friends among both conservative and revolutionary leaders, with the firmest of all being the modern merchants and the new student class.

If useful services and the temporary provision of leadership had been the entire extent of the Association's work, they would still appear in perspective as a genuine pioneering contribution to social reform. But the organization played a greater role in reform. Because of its roots in Western Christianity, and particularly because of its emphasis in the United States on service, the organization brought to China a concern for social welfare. During the final years of the Ch'ing era, that concern was translated into action. At first Western personnel rather than Chinese members took the lead, by broadening the public lectures originally devoted to science and religion to include talks about welfare, government, and health. A few student members, however, became interested in the type of social service that Harlan Beach had described. Under the guidance of the Association they made tentative moves to help the poor, the illiterate, and the neglected in their communities. Although the lectures and the student work were unrelated, the Association bore within itself the means to integrate them into a new dynamic for carrying on broad community welfare programs. Thus, as a republican China came into being, so did a small sense of urban community responsibility. Its growth was to have profound effects on the country.

The Association could not have performed such a multitude of services without allies outside its own membership. Fortunately, the organization had sunk roots at a time when it could legitimately share both traditional and modern values with the Chinese. The epitome of modern reform as envisioned in 1900, the Association's prescriptions for reform were nevertheless not destructive. As its Western personnel gained experience, they emphasized that they did not want to bring about a collision of two cultures—could not, in fact, for they sensed that China would accept Western civilization only on Chinese terms. What Gailey, Brockman, Lewis, and later arrivals aimed for was a cultural exchange, a subtle blending of institutions and ideas. Any Western idea, they believed, would have to find a naturally fertile Chinese soil in which to take root, or it would die.[14] They perceived with considerable sophistication that if social change were to be adopted voluntarily, it would have to proceed from the familiar to the unfamiliar through the mediation of shared values. Thus, they took pains to relate their ideas to those already familiar in China, to continue indigenizing the organization, and to echo Chinese ideals wherever possible.

Many secretaries chose to intimate that Association ideas and values were by no means completely alien to China and were, indeed, the Western counterpart of that ancient and honored tradition, the Confucian ethic. It was by no means mere expediency to detect similarities between Confucian ideas and those of the Association, for points of basic agreement existed. In the linked concepts of morality as the core of a great society and of education as the means to achieving that morality, Association secretaries could agree with Confucian scholars. Thus, for working purposes there were enough similarities to make for compatibility.

The dismaying disintegration of old values and customs during these years deeply concerned thoughtful Chinese. To those seeking a way to transmit China's moral essence, the possibility of finding an acceptable substitute for traditional Confucianism was tempting. The scholar Yen Fu, groping for a moral center to the modern world, told one Association secretary that young students no longer believed in anything and affirmed his own belief in the need for religious or moral instruction in the schools.[15] About the country, other individuals sought to fashion a modern morality. Yuan Shih-k'ai's army reportedly adopted the slogan "mind, body and spirit" in approximately the Association's sense, although the roots for the slogan lay far in the Confucian past.[16] Businessmen interviewed by Fletcher Brockman seemed to comprehend easily his pleas for a morally-based institution for the young.[17]

Clearly, non-Christian Chinese and the Y.M.C.A. shared a value system with little strain to either, and the Association took full advantage of this happy situation. For example, in phrases from an appeal to a Shanghai taotai for help in securing land for an Association building, Robert Lewis described Association aims as "to clean the heart and make the character true and strong, and to teach principles of loyalty, fidelity, generosity, kindness and self-respect, love to God and love to man . . . in short, to make capable and loyal citizens for China." [18] There was an even clearer Confucian appeal in an address made by the secretary William Lockwood when welcoming to the Shanghai Association the Manchu Tuan-fang, at the time viceroy of Liang-kiang. The Association directed itself to a threefold concern, explained Lockwood: the mind, the body, and the heart of young men. Inasmuch as China's greatest sage had maintained that rectifying the heart was the basis of a country's greatness, he continued, it was now necessary to rectify the hearts of China's coming generation. The Association hoped that all three aspects of man's nature could be "rectified, balanced and harmonized into one complete and perfect manhood." [19]

To allay further the fears of traditional Chinese that Christian backing might render the Association a threat, the organization continued to soft-pedal its outward religious manifestations, although religious work remained a part of the program. In Shanghai, Robert Lewis left the characters *chi-tu* (Jesus) off the Association's door, much to the dismay of Willard Lyon.[20] In 1902, when the word "College" was dropped from the official title in recognition of the Association's expanded aims, so was the phrase *Yu-t'u* or "disciple" with its pietistic connotation. The official title of the Association was thenceforth *Chi-tu Chiao Ch'ing-nien hui* or Protestant Christian Youth Association, but it was familiarly known only as *Ch'ing-nien hui* or Youth Association, without the religious prefix. The term "Ch'ing-nien" connoted the youth who were sons of gentry or wealthy merchants.[21] To further the attempt to echo Chinese values, the Association continued to encourage Chinese leadership. At the 1901 Nanking convention, for instance, 139 Chinese and 39 Westerners were present. In 1901 there were three Chinese employees; in 1907, sixteen. As Chinese nationalism grew, such actions became increasingly important for an imported institution.

Its sympathy for Chinese aspirations and ideals, both traditional and new, won the Y.M.C.A. a ready welcome among
different groups with differing objectives. Thus, between 1900
and 1907 it forged alliances with each of China's urban elites.
Some of these alliances were stronger than others, but taken
together, they assured the young organization important backing.

Early relationships between the Association and official
China were meager, coming about through sentimental personal ties. T'ang Shao-yi, familiar with America and American
institutions because of his experience as a Yung Wing boy,
was probably the first official friend of the Association. As
early as 1896 or 1897 he cast himself in the role of informal
adviser to the Tientsin group, dispensing such bits of advice as
a warning not to use the word *hui* or "society" in their title
because it connoted conspiracy and sedition to the uneasy
imperial government.[22] As T'ang's star rose, his friendship and
support for the Association continued. There are no specific
records of his early work on behalf of the group besides
providing financial help, but unquestionably his friendship
was an asset, for it never hurt to know an official in China.
The general need for support from officials was borne in on
Western secretaries as the necessity for acquiring money,
prestige, and title to land became more pressing. Thus, the
Association was eager to help officials whenever the paths of
the two groups should cross, and as a result its circle of
acquaintances enlarged.

There are not many specific names in the records, for like
other Westerners writing home, Association correspondents
often alluded to their Chinese friends merely by title or status,
as "one of the top officials in the town" or "the late Viceroy's
nephew." The names mentioned, however, are revealing. Yen

Hsiu of Tientsin, for example, figured prominently in the destinies of the Association. He was one of Tzu Hsi's advisers until he took the part of the reformers during the Hundred Days of Reform, and he subsequently retired temporarily from public life.[23] He was primarily attracted by the Association's work in education. Later the names appeared of Liang Tun-yen, another Yung Wing boy, and of Wu T'ing-fang and Alfred Sze of the foreign office.[24] Tuan-fang, the part-Manchu official prominent in the early reform movement, often lent strong support.[25] The taotai who led the Anglo-American boycott in Shanghai in 1905 was a firm friend, making a donation to the land fund for an Association building at the same time that he was involved in the boycott.[26] The most revealing aspect of the list, therefore, is its diversity. Officials supporting the Association appear to have been a mixed bag, with their only common denominator being their reform-minded cast rather than a highly conservative bent.

Chinese officials turned to the Association for a number of reasons. There was a sentimental attachment on the part of some. Diplomats used it to promote international amity. For the officials who had no apparent connection through sentiment or foreign ties, the motivation seems to have been both ideological and material. Ideologically, the Association stressed its role of providing for the young men of China a sane, moderate, and moral basis, as shown in its letters to the Shanghai taotai and to Tuan-fang. To official China, such objectives were a welcome contrast to the exclusively radical political aims of other associations of young students and literati burgeoning throughout the country. The cities of China were seething with unrest. In his autobiography Chiang Mon-lin recalled strikes in Nanyang, at his mission school in Hangchow, and throughout the country in government schools. By 1903 Chekiang Provincial College was "deluged," he wrote, by revolutionary material shipped in from Japan, which was devoured by students at the college.[27] Conspiracy flourished in Shanghai under the protection of the treaty system.[28] In contrast, the association provided an institution for young men that was not only nonpolitical but also based on a morality of which official China could approve. As Wu T'ing-fang put it a few years later, the Y.M.C.A. helped its members by providing moral teaching and innocent amusement.[29] It is reasonable to conclude that official China hoped the Association might divert the energies of China's youth into safer channels.

In addition, the Association provided material services that were not necessarily governmental functions but were helpful to officials in their struggle to modernize. The Association's own educational work performed a genuine stop-gap service. Association personnel also participated informally in the scientific and educational programs of the government. Furthermore, they helped students overseas. The Shanghai Association established a bureau to assist students going abroad by providing passport information and letters of introduction.[30] Associations in the United States detailed men to meet students at the docks and shield them from the indignities besetting Chinese at customs and immigration counters.[31] The Chinese Association established a special branch in Tokyo, which carried on full-fledged student work after 1906.

Thus, the Association ingratiated itself with the official hierarchy in many ways. As an added bonus, many young men who were Association members and had some grasp of modern affairs became secretaries and aides to a number of high officials after about 1905.[32] As time passed, the Association developed a cordial if not a close relationship with a growing number of officials.

With businessmen, the Association had not just a cordial relationship but an intimate one. Between the Chinese business community and the Chinese Y.M.C.A. stretched strong bonds, for the older businessmen were the financial keystone of the Association program, and in turn the Association provided financial, social, and educational advantages not readily available elsewhere in those early years.

The most natural bond was with those Chinese businessmen who were Christian themselves, as illustrated in at least two cases. Wang Kok-shan, briefly a commissioner for the Shanghai-Nanking Railway (1906) and then business manager for the Han Yeh P'ing Iron Works, was a pastor's son who served as president of the Tientsin Association early in its existence. The Yung Wing boy Tong Kai-son, who moved from the K'ai P'ing Mining Company to presidency of the Venus Life Insurance Company to appointment as the first president of Tsing Hua College, was treasurer of the Shanghai Association for five years. Chinese Christian businessmen, however, were not usually well-to-do and never represented an important factor in the Association. Fortunately, non-Christian businessmen were sufficiently enthusiastic to provide the necessary support.

The Association appealed to those businessmen for a number of reasons. A major reason emerges from the following list of names signed to a letter sent to the Shanghai Municipal Council in 1906 protesting public gambling booths during spring Race Week, such protests also being one of Robert Lewis' peripheral activities:

Shen Tun-ho (Commissioner, Shanghai-Nanking Railway)
Wong Kok-shan (Commissioner, Shanghai-Nanking Railway)
Chu Pao-san (head of the Chinese Chamber of Commerce)
Chu Yu-chee (Director, China Merchants' Steam Navigation Co.)

Lee Yuen-see (merchant)

Chun Fai-ting (Manager, China Merchants' Steam Navigation Co.)

Soo Pao-san (merchant)

Woo Saw-ching (comprador, Arnold, Karberg and Co., also listed as Woo Sam-hin)

Wong Soong Dong (comprador, U.S. Consulate General) [33]

To many of the men on this list, with its overtones of international trade, the primary appeal of the Association was that it spelled profit. Shanghai was booming, and Chinese enterprises were multiplying. In response, the Association plunged into part-time vocational education, and by 1905 was giving classes in bookkeeping, arithmetic, document translation, French, English, Mandarin, Japanese, and music, with Esperanto and photography in the offing. Association-trained men represented a source of competent help for merchants setting up their own organizations to carry on foreign trade. Tuan-fang asserted to a visiting American, Ernest Burton, that mission schools were good only for preparing men for business, decidedly not for official life.[34] As Western subjects constituted the core of Association work, the trained personnel thus produced were valuable to modern business.

There were, however, less tangible appeals for the older businessmen. An aura of power and status radiated from the Shanghai Association. At one of the earliest fund-raising meetings, for instance, guests of honor were not only the aforementioned Chu Pao-san, but also Count Portalis, head of the Paris Y.M.C.A., and S. W. Woodward, a department store mogul and head of the Washington, D.C., Y.M.C.A.[35] American businessmen visiting China to drum up trade were likely to have a connection with the Association in their home towns. A prominent Baltimore industrialist named Joshua Levering talked to Nanking businessmen about the Association at Fletcher Brockman's request; John Wanamaker poured a fortune into buildings in China, Korea, and Japan. Fletcher Brockman came to know through personal contact or correspondence a virtual Who's Who of American business tycoons: the Colgates, the McCormicks, and even Henry Ford.[36] Chinese businessmen, noted for their astuteness, were surely aware of the influential links of the Association.[37] Tuan-fang, for instance, knew that in the United States John Mott had the sympathetic ear of John D. Rockefeller, Jr.[38] It may be surmised that the exceptionally high prestige of businessmen in the United States supported the egos of Chinese merchants, who were long accustomed to an inferior social status, and that Chinese businessmen considered it a source of potential good will and perhaps even good business to support an Association with such powerful ties.

In addition, the Association for a time served the familiar purpose of providing protective cover for merchants who desired reform but were still unsure of the risks involved in leadership. At least once in the early years, a secretary trying to start work in Nanking reported that he was approached by members of a guild who wanted to pledge financial support and membership in return for the protection the Association could afford them under the treaty system.[39] Moreover, Chinese businessmen were concerned about their own sons, some of whom were presumably worrying them by their odd fads and restless behavior. Accordingly, Shanghai businessmen were ready to talk about reform for hours with the willing Association personnel.[40]

Above all, young businessmen clearly liked the Association. The vocational training offered in part-time classes was extremely important to them, for as Fletcher Brockman put it, an Association training meant higher wages.[41] Since the new government schools springing up in the country did not provide part-time vocational work, for a while the Association had the field to itself. Shanghai secretary William Lockwood could thus write in 1905, "These classes interest the best classes of men in the city, compradores, managers of business houses as well as some of the student class who are college graduates." [42] The promise of additional profit was attractive, as was the employment bureau set up by the Association as a clearing house for jobs, which was in operation in 1910 and possibly earlier.

There were other tangible advantages for young members in the tea rooms, game rooms, dark rooms, libraries, showers, and moderately priced dormitories that were promised in the new headquarters. But in the final analysis, they were probably balanced by nonmaterial appeals. Here, at last, was a *hui* or "society" for young businessmen where they need not take a back seat either to their elders or to young men of superior social status; a place where they could be free from the restrictions of age and hierarchy.[43]

Thus, links were formed by the Y.M.C.A. with the emerging modern sector. But in the midst of the success with these groups, Fletcher Brockman had by no means forgotten the Association's original aim in going to China, that of making friends with traditional students. While the courtship with businessmen continued, therefore, he attempted to expand student work. Because of the Boxer Uprising, such work had taken a step backward. Modern education in Tientsin was virtually annihilated, since only the medical school survived the fighting, and the Association building itself lay in ruins.

Gailey rented quarters in the French Concession, where he started classes and lectures for students as well as businessmen. In Shanghai, student work received no special attention except as it shared in the general services of the Association. Only in mission schools, therefore, did the Association have any widespread student contact in 1901, with forty student Associations theoretically in operation. These, however, barely figure in the annals of the time, for a college secretary was never appointed to visit them systematically, although Willard Lyon concerned himself generally with student work.[44] Brockman was fully aware that mission school students did not represent the mainstream of China. It was a matter of real concern to him that students working for the traditional examinations as well as students in the new government schools must somehow be reached, to say nothing of the older literati.

In 1901, therefore, soon after the Boxer Uprising, Fletcher Brockman began to work seriously with Timothy Richard on the problem of reaching traditional students. The atmosphere seemed promising, for the upper classes were aware of the need for modern education, and some were turning to the Association for help. Robert Gailey reported a new and friendly air in Tientsin; [45] Robert Lewis remarked that he was invited night after night to give counsel at "the wealthiest Confucian homes in Shanghai." [46] Timothy Richard became more firmly convinced than ever that science was the only approach to the literati, both young and adult.[47] It was time for action, he declared, in which the Association should take the lead, for no formal church group was planning any major program for the literati. When John Mott returned to China at the end of 1901, he agreed to cooperate in finding men specially suited to work with the literati. Although he resisted

Richard's suggestion that the Association focus all its energies on science lectures, he agreed to divert some resources to that purpose immediately.

The model was to be the small but thriving museum-lecture program set up in Tsingchow by Richard's old friend J. S. Whitewright. Toward the end of 1902 Brockman made a five-week trip to Tsingchow to visit Whitewright's museum, which by then also contained a reading room and a science lecture hall. Whitewright and his Chinese assistants had been giving lectures for several years on a variety of subjects, including the steam engine, motions of the earth, the telegraph, eclipses, flood control on the Yellow Sea, and Western education. The interest of literati and officials in the museum opened the way for establishing lectures on science, on political and educational subjects, and finally on Christianity. In addition, Whitewright and his assistants gave completely secular lectures to students who went to Tsingchow for their examinations. The Tsingchow experiment had proved so successful that duplicate work was started at the provincial college in Tsinan, the provincial capital, where it was flourishing. The student lectures, reported Whitewright, attracted thousands.[48]

Brockman was impressed, despite what he considered the overly secular emphasis of the lectures and the fact that all support for the effort came from abroad. He took careful note of Whitewright's approach. Literati interest, Whitewright emphasized, reflected not only the content of the lectures but also the spirit and personality of the lecturers. Whitewright's main principle was "the cordial recognition of the good in China and the Chinese as against an attitude that dwells mainly on the evils and faults of the Chinese and is unfriendly and unsympathetic."[49]

Brockman decided that the Association might well adapt the

Whitewright technique on a larger scale. First, he attempted to persuade Whitewright himself or the president of the Tsinan college, Dr. William Hayes, to join the Association for work with the literati.[50] Neither would come, but Hayes's assistant, a graduate of Tengchow College named Chung Wei-yi, joined the Tientsin Association. Chung not only had the benefit of scientific training because of Calvin Mateer's influence at the college, but as a result of Mateer's insistence on instruction in Chinese, Chung had also learned the classics well enough to acquire a Chinese degree. As a scholar himself, Chung was acceptable to other scholars, and he proved a real asset.[51]

There was thought of starting literati work using Gailey, but Gailey was not a trained scientist. In the United States, therefore, John Mott searched for someone who was a professional scientist, a personable lecturer, a dedicated Christian, and a Y.M.C.A. member. He singled out Clarence Hovey Robertson, professor of mechanical engineering at Purdue University. Robertson's photographs show a pleasant-looking young man with a shock of curly hair parted in the middle, according to the style of the times, and with the serious expression common to college yearbook photographs. The seriousness, however, was accompanied by a good deal of fire both intellectual and religious. He was not a minister, for already the Association was recruiting from laymen instead. He had become an instructor at Purdue after acquiring degrees from that university in 1895 and 1896. As a classroom teacher, he possessed considerable experience in science demonstration and was familiar with the departmental museum, which had a supply of steam engines and other mechanical equipment. By 1901 he was treasurer of the student Y.M.C.A. advisory board at the university, and his wife was secretary. He also was a letter man in football and track and held the Purdue record of 109 feet 2 inches for the sixteen-pound hammer throw, abilities that were by no means irrelevant to his later work.[52]

Mott, a compelling persuader, influenced Robertson to leave Purdue and go to China as the pioneer scientific worker for the Association. After Robertson and his wife arrived in China in December 1902, the National Committee sent them to Nanking so that Robertson could deliver a series of lectures on science and religion to the students scheduled to assemble there in 1903 for the triennial examinations. Tientsin was unavailable for the experiment, since cities involved in the Boxer Uprising were forbidden to hold examinations for five years, and Brockman also felt that it was time to explore the possibilities of developing work in other cities. Encouraged by Brockman, and advised by a few reform-minded Chinese, Robertson began to plan a series of vivid lectures.[53]

At the same time, Brockman was at work on large-scale plans that he wanted John Mott to appraise and finance. Brockman recognized that any meaningful attempt to reach students must cover more of the country than a single city or province. He therefore presented to Mott a plan for a science center in each inland capital of China. Each center would have a library, science lecture hall, laboratory, museum, and assembly hall at an estimated total cost of about $25,000 per city. The centers would serve as points of influence from which Western knowledge could radiate.[54] This program represented a more ambitious version of the Whitewright work and of Gilbert Reid's old plans, which were still hanging fire.[55]

While these schemes were being transmitted to the United States, Robertson's Nanking campaign for the examination period was reaching an impasse, which he later ascribed to official reluctance to countenance any activity that might stir up the students.[56] He decided, however, to offer lectures for persons other than the traditional students, for which he sent admission tickets to selected groups of literati, officials, teachers, and students in modern schools, on the advice of Timothy Richard and missionary A. P. Parker. Response was good. Not only did about a hundred teachers in the new government schools attend one demonstration, as he reported, but they brought uninvited a great number of students, including the sons of the viceroy.[57] A few months' work convinced Robertson that for him the lecture technique was effective. With characteristic exuberance he worked on his language studies, dreamed of a lecture program that would blanket the country, and sent lengthy memoranda to the United States urging action. As these events unrolled, however, circumstances in Tientsin were already conspiring to move him there to continue his lecture experiments, for work with the upper classes in that city had taken an unexpectedly rewarding turn.

As the smoke cleared from Tientsin in 1901, the city found itself without an educational system. Forbidden to hold examinations for five years, absolutely without elementary or middle schools, and with most of its modern colleges wiped out, it faced the necessity of taking immediate action for its young people. Mission schools were of course available, but the gentry of Tientsin were not interested in turning their sons over to schools where exposure to the foreign religion was mandatory. Furthermore, mission school graduates were not accredited by the government. The gentry looked elsewhere for help.

It was now that the previous work of the Tientsin Association and the personality of its secretaries began to bear fruit. Specifically, Robert Gailey already enjoyed a reputation as a likable, competent young man who respected Chinese values, Chinese dignity, and Chinese capacity for leadership.[58] In 1901 Charles Tenney, president of the temporarily defunct

Tientsin university, approached Gailey with news that some gentry families had decided to open a new modern school for their teenage sons. They had taken over a battered government examination hall in the Chinese city and had begun to repair it for use as a temporary school, to be called the P'u T'ung or General School. Tenney brought to Gailey an invitation from the gentry to help organize the school. They would pay the expenses, and Gailey would have a free hand in picking English teachers. Their eagerness to present him with acceptable terms was obvious. In disregard of the imperial government's wishes, they promised to make the performance of Confucian rites in the school optional. Gailey, delighted at a chance to reach the long inaccessible literati and to work in the Chinese city, agreed to start a school without giving any religious instruction. Thus began the first high school in Tientsin, probably the third or fourth in the country.[59] Over a hundred sons of literati families were quickly enrolled. Gailey taught English and organized a staff to teach science and the Chinese classics. The gentry soon allowed him to start a voluntary Sunday Bible class. The chief value of the work, he wrote, was that it was helping him at last to meet and form a bond with the literati. At the same time he started a separate school for children of businessmen.[60]

Installing Gailey as head of the P'u T'ung School was a clear example of the Chinese willingness to make a practical compromise in the face of necessity, provided their values were not seriously threatened. They needed Gailey's leadership for a short time and his teaching skills for even longer. By 1903, official schools were opening in the province under the efficient and widespread educational program of Yuan Shih-k'ai. The government then pre-empted the examination hall headquarters and established there a middle school. By 1905,

Gailey reported, there were at least fifty government schools in the vicinity, more or less tuition free. Clearly, the Chinese intended to take over development of their own institutions whenever possible. The sponsors of the P'u T'ung School, however, did not abandon Gailey. They helped him to move the school closer to the re-established central Association headquarters, paid the first year's rent, and furnished the rooms. Gailey now turned the school into a regular full-time Association school with optional religious instruction.[61] Although the school charged a substantial fee, there was always a long waiting list, and most of the hundred and fifty students enrolled came from gentry families. Relations with government schools were cordial, too, for Gailey taught at the Tientsin Middle School that had displaced him.[62]

While the government system was developing, a few private schools were also emerging. One was started by Gailey's assistant Chung Wei-yi, who founded what was thought to be the first girls' school in the Chinese city. Far more important was the help Gailey gave to Chang Po-ling, who was attempting to establish first-class private education in the city. Chang, not long graduated from the Tientsin Naval Academy, had turned his back on naval service to become a tutor to the children of Yen Hsiu. In 1903 Yen Hsiu and Chang made a trip to Japan to investigate educational practices there. On their return they expanded the small tutorial group Chang had been teaching into a regular middle school. When Chang appealed for help in finding Western instructors for the new school, Gailey, his wife, and Stanley Wright of the customs office offered to teach there, an action that further enhanced relations with important men in the community.[63]

That the patronage of men such as Yen and Chang was helpful soon became clear. As the number of government schools increased, so did the official determination to eradicate Christian influence. Worship of the tablets of Confucius was obligatory in government schools, and in 1904 teaching of any view but Confucianism in them was officially forbidden.[64] Since such stipulations were difficult for Christians to meet, both missionaries and many Chinese Christian teachers began to resign from official schools. Yet despite these decrees, in 1905 the Chihli Bureau of Education granted the P'u T'ung School official recognition, a privilege probably related to the appointment of Yen Hsiu that year to the vice-presidency of the imperial board of education in Peking. According to several accounts, Gailey's school was the only Christian-related school to achieve such status during Ch'ing times. Recognition meant that students were invited to participate in public functions, that they carried on required military drill, and that they passed in public review with other schools. Gailey wrote that his students were accepted into many of the rebuilt government schools and that Chinese officials asked to have the school staff included at viceregal functions. There was no official of any importance, he wrote, who did not know of the school's work.[65] In public and private, officials acknowledged the Association as a pioneer of the new education in the city, and they backed up their praise with support. In 1904, 95 percent of the annual budget came from non-Christians.[66]

The story of this early educational work reveals many significant themes. The very existence of the P'u T'ung School, of course, was important, not only because it filled a gap lasting about two years when no other secular high school education was available in Tientsin, but also because the quality of its instruction challenged the Chinese to set high standards. The cordial relationship with the gentry, although relatively transitory, helped strengthen the Tientsin Association and provided a hospitable environment for other work soon afterward. Most important in the chain of social reform, perhaps, was the assistance Gailey afforded Chang Po-ling. Gailey was only the first of several Association secretaries to teach at Chang's school: C. H. Robertson was on hand after 1905 to teach physics, and Roscoe M. Hersey, who arrived in 1905, also taught there. This cooperation helped the new school to present an attractive curriculum, a factor that led directly to its expansion as the Nankai Middle School and later as the justly famous Nankai University. Chang Po-ling stands in Chinese history as the father of modern private schooling in the country, and the help he got from the Tientsin Association played a part in his success. Furthermore, he played a part in the success of the Association too, for the close collaboration ensured Chang's warm cooperation and put into motion a series of events that led to Chang's conversion to Christianity, his presidency of the Tientsin Association, and his powerful work in behalf of the organization for the rest of his life.

By 1905, Gailey's work in Tientsin, Lewis's in Shanghai, and Robertson's in Nanking had created considerable sentiment for expansion to other cities, and events in China that year reinforced the general optimism of Association personnel. Not only had the Japanese victory in the Russo-Japanese War intensified China's attempts to modernize, but there came the welcome news that the examination system had abruptly been abolished. It was, wrote Minister W. W. Rockhill to the U.S. State Department, a step capable of shaking society to its foundations.[67] With the change, a tidal wave of students was expected to flow into government schools. When Robert Gailey heard the news, he remarked, "now the problem of the literati has dissolved into that of the modern student." [68] An Association effort to reach the modern student seemed more important than ever. Furthermore, the rising flood of students pouring into Japan presented a new challenge. With a combination of foresight and luck, Association secretaries were able to meet these new circumstances, for they managed to find a number of interests in common with the "new literati" and to be in the right places at the right time to share those interests. The next five years further improved Association-student relationships.

The first proving ground was Tientsin, as it had been for Willard Lyon only ten years before. In 1905 Robert Gailey was due for a furlough, and Robertson was assigned to Tientsin, partly to pinch-hit and partly to receive further administrative training. Tientsin would soon need a new head secretary, for Gailey was shortly to begin devoting part of his time to Peking. Princeton University, in line with the fashion for an American university to take on a project in China (as did Yale and Oberlin) had decided to form a group known as "Princeton in Peking" that would sponsor and staff an Association in that city. John Wanamaker had already promised to donate fifty thousand dollars for a building, and Gailey was picked as the proper man to head the new Association, since he was not only influential with the upper classes but was also a Princeton graduate.[69] Robertson moved reluctantly, for assignment to a specific city seemed to him to spell the end of any immediate hopes to set up a countrywide museum or lecture system—proposals that at any rate had failed to generate widespread support in the United States. In Tientsin, however, he found that the arrival of another secretary, R. M. Hersey, left Robertson more time for creative work.

At once Robertson set to work to test the power of science lectures in a new environment. Gailey himself had been in touch with Whitewright and had started a tiny museum full of natural history specimens and engineering models made in the Whitewright shop. Chung Wei-yi was giving science lectures. Unlike the past, however, the Association was no longer alone in modern work. Already Chinese unaffiliated with the Association were giving science lectures, just as Chinese not affiliated with the Association had established four excellent reading rooms, opened a lecture hall in the Chinese city, and begun to give part-time classes modeled after Association work. "We'll have to do what they can't," observed Gailey, and it became clear that the Association must now excel in the old fields or pioneer in new ones.[70] Fortunately, Robertson was qualified to do both.

Both as science lecturer and as mechanical tinkerer, Robertson was pre-eminent in Tientsin over the next few years. His training, which had been first-class, was still up-to-date. Thus, he wrote, a group trying to run a science museum in a former Taoist monastery turned to him for help, for although they possessed an extensive collection of educational and scientific equipment, they lacked competent men to make repairs, which he was able to do. As time went on, he helped the army with its wireless telegraph and the medical college (I-hsüeh t'ang) with its X-ray apparatus, and in turn the government museum offered him unqualified use of its equipment.[71] More important for the student work, however, were his gifts as a lecturer. A later associate remembered Robertson as "Big Robbie: inventor, scientist, revivalist, athlete, Barnum!"[72] His sense of theater seems to have been formidable, for years later Chinese would report to him that they still remembered his lectures. The combination of professional competence and stage presence gave his lecture series immediate popularity. Government schools sent students twice a week to Association buildings to hear lectures by him or by the Chinese assistants he was training.[73] The lectures he gave for teachers from the government schools also attracted men from the provincial board of education. Gailey had at first been unsure of the power of public lectures, but after watching Robertson in action, he became thoroughly convinced of their effectiveness as a technique for stirring audiences.[74]

In the course of his work, Robertson came to know Chang Po-ling, who induced him to teach physics at the Nankai Middle School. The two men developed a profoundly affectionate mutual regard, especially after they discovered a common concern for spiritual matters. Robertson began to explore with Chang the ramifications of Christianity, which eventually led to Chang's decision to become a Christian in 1908. In terms of their public lives and their interest in students, however, another mutual enthusiasm was more immediately pertinent, for both men were eager to introduce organized sports to Chinese students.

Western athletics had not enjoyed a successful history in China. Intense competitive activity was alien to the upper classes: when an effort was made to introduce football at the Tientsin Naval Academy late in the nineteenth century, the directors prohibited it, remarking that the sport was unworthy of a gentleman.[75] The story went the rounds in Shanghai of a Chinese gentleman who, while watching four Americans play tennis, inquired why they didn't hire someone else to do it for them.[76] Chiang Mon-lin thought as a child that his teachers were trying to squeeze the life out of him by forbidding him to run or play outside.[77]

After the Sino-Japanese War, a few officials began to emphasize physical fitness for military personnel. German instructors started to train Yuan Shih-k'ai's modern army in calisthenics, and military drill was introduced into a few schools, among them the Tientsin university, where Willard

Lyon began to instruct students. In 1901 Liu K'un-i and Chang Chih-tung recommended extending drill to other schools, and in 1903 plans for the modern school system included three hours a week of physical exercise from the first through the fifth grades.[78] These efforts, however, did not include body contact sports or violent competitive activity. They were confined to mission schools. Chang Po-ling believed in sports, but in the earliest years of the school had neither space nor staff to carry on athletic work.

Of all the Western innovations Robert Gailey had thought suitable for Chinese students, only parlor games seemed more incongruous than competitive sports. Nevertheless, in 1902 he wangled room for sports in the Austrian concession, laid out an athletic field, and proclaimed an athletic meet, which became an almost annual event, though of little initial importance.[79] By 1904 he had persuaded Association members to play football with Western soldiers, a matter of some pride to him because, although the Chinese were badly beaten, they at least agreed to play. These activities, however, did not formally include any of the government or private schools in Tientsin.[80]

As a star athlete, Robertson was pressed into service to coach track events at the P'u T'ung School. There it became clear that the ardor he brought to religion and to science encompassed sports as well, and communicated itself to others. When Chang Po-ling moved the Nankai Middle School to larger quarters in 1907, Robertson laid out a playing field on the school grounds and systematically developed an athletic program, which proved even more popular than his science lectures. At the Association's Fifth Annual Meet in 1907, both Chang and Robertson collaborated in urging the students to greater athletic activity. Plans had been started in Asian

102

Y.M.C.A.'s to hold a Far Eastern Olympics, since the Japanese had shown considerable proficiency in Western sports. At the 1907 meet Chang delivered a stirring speech about the spirit of the Greek Olympics and the nature of their modern counterpart.[81] Robertson then challenged the students to produce contenders for a Far Eastern Olympics.[82] With national spirit daily growing stronger, the Tientsin student community responded enthusiastically. As 1907 wore on, the government schools to whom Robertson gave science lectures asked him to coach athletics as well. Athletics proved to be even more appealing to the young than science lectures. Furthermore, the Shanghai Association was showing that young businessmen liked sports as well as young students did, for its members were not only riding bicycles and playing tennis but had formed a baseball team to play the Japanese (who won with a score, it was noted, that looked like the Russian war debt).[83] The introduction of sports, with its unexpected popularity, was yet another intrinsically valuable service performed by the Y.M.C.A. for China, both for its unmistakable physical benefits and for the sense of pride in performance it developed in young Chinese. Without question the Y.M.C.A. was the founder of modern physical education in China.

Important as this might be in Tientsin and Shanghai, however, and despite Robertson's scientific program, to carry on student work in only two cities did not constitute a widespread effort. The Nankai Middle School started a student Association in 1904, and the Shanghai Polytechnic Institute (Ko-chih Shu-yüan) began one in 1906, but elsewhere modern students remained untouched by the organization. Even if the Association had had ample funds and trained personnel, government hostility would still have kept it out of most schools. In Tokyo, however, students from all over China were meeting free of the restraints of the imperial government and of a Confucian society. There, in 1906, the Association determined to go.

The end of the examination system had opened the flood-gates to study abroad, somewhat to France and the United States, but mostly to Japan. By 1906, according to Association information, there were at least thirteen thousand Chinese students in Japan, 98 percent of them being in Tokyo. All provinces but Kansu were represented. Japan was not ready to receive such a throng into her schools, in part because few of the Chinese students understood Japanese. Several profes-sional and liberal arts schools were set up specifically for the Chinese, and a few Japanese institutions established compe-tent courses for the new arrivals, but hundreds of opportunists also set up fly-by-night schools where students could get a "rapid" education. Ill-educated, ill-housed, awkward in the new surroundings, often received with hostility, Chinese students, even the serious ones, found it hard to adjust. Apart from the lurid attractions of Tokyo, their social life was usually con-fined to the provincial student clubs that they formed.[84]

At the end of 1905, Willard Lyon and a Tientsin secretary named Chang Pei-chih went to Tokyo to make a survey. They talked with missionaries, Chinese students, and Japanese edu-cators, besides reading the publications of the press and of the students themselves. There was, Lyon reported, a challenging opportunity to serve and influence the students through the familiar Association program of education and recreation. Deeply committed to the religious aspects of the Association, Lyon had listened to students with dismay. Many, he wrote, were encountering a sudden and shallow introduction to the great ideas of the world, which was making them hot-headed and in some cases revolutionary. More and more they scoffed at the need for a religious foundation to society, be it Confu-

cianism or Christianity, for Japan, they maintained, had risen
to power without religion. On the other hand, wrote Lyon, "the
spirit of religious liberty pervading Japan has influenced the
Chinese students in the direction of open-mindedness to all
truth." [85] This meant they would at least listen to a new
religious message. So ill at ease were they in their surroundings that the man who could speak to them in their own
tongue and counsel them in a kindly way—the man who
would be a brother to them—might hope to win them. He
ended:

> The possible future influence of these students is immeas-
> urable. They come from all parts of the Empire. Thousands
> of them will become school-teachers in the towns and vil-
> lages of China, hundreds will rise to professorships in the
> higher institutions, and not a few will some day hold posi-
> tions of national influence. Experience has shown that the
> students of the government colleges are a strategically im-
> portant and exceedingly hopeful field for Christian effort. In
> them are found at an impressionable age the future leaders
> of the country. In China, however, the modern government
> college is, at the present time, practically inaccessible to
> Christian influence. Tokyo furnishes the key to this closed
> door.[86]

In collaboration with several church groups, the Association
decided to send a staff to Tokyo, and early in 1906, J. M.
Clinton and C. T. Wang (Wang Cheng-ting) sailed for Japan.
Clinton was a newly arrived American secretary. In Wang,
Fletcher Brockman thought he had found the wise Chinese
counselor whom the students could trust. Wang was a graduate of the Tientsin Naval Academy, the son of a Ningpo
preacher, and an early member of the Tientsin Y.M.C.A.

Brockman wrote of him: "He is in many respects the most promising young Chinese I have ever met . . . alert, a good organizer, almost idolized by the students who come in close contact with him, and . . . deeply spiritual." A native of Chekiang, Wang knew Mandarin, Cantonese, Fukienese, and English. Brockman saw in him a potential leader and therefore wanted to keep him in Association work, for as Brockman observed with prescience, "The foreigners in China must rapidly take a second place . . . it behooves us to get ready for this quickly." [87]

Using the Japanese Y.M.C.A. as headquarters and collaborating with the local missionaries, Wang and Clinton enrolled three hundred Chinese in evening educational classes, started a series of lectures on science, religion, and patriotism, opened a reading room, and inaugurated a social recreation program.[88] When Brockman visited Tokyo in October 1906, he received a warm endorsement of the work from prominent Japanese, notably Count Okuma, whose Waseda University had enrolled six hundred Chinese students and was expecting more. Brockman enthusiastically decided to send more secretaries to Tokyo. "Here things are wide open to our influence and these men will run the colleges and the government of China within a few years," he wrote to John Mott.[89]

In Tokyo, the Association realized, it was functioning in a milieu far different from that on the mainland, for student talk in Japan was not of education or athletics but of politics. In Tientsin and Shanghai, secretaries heard discussion of reform, but in Tokyo the talk was of political revolution. The T'ung-meng hui had been officially formed in September 1905, and its revolutionary journal *Min Pao* began publication in February 1906. The Association was troubled over how to establish a relationship with students whose minds were on

military coups, since the Y.M.C.A. was deliberately nonpolitical. Half a century earlier in the United States, sharp debates
over slavery had split local Associations into Northern and
Southern groups, which almost shattered the unity of the
movement, and ever since the Association had avoided political discussion. This hesitancy was even stronger abroad,
where secretaries were especially sensitive to the vulnerability
of a foreign movement and afraid to back the wrong horse. In
China, although their hearts were with the modernizers and
they felt little sympathy for the anti-Christian, conservative
Ch'ing government, such opinions were not to be expressed
aloud.[90]

Some of this caution spilled over into the Tokyo Association,
where secretaries were not inclined to approve discussion of
violent blood baths and explosive revolutions.[91] In public, C. T.
Wang went about as far as possible for a spokesman of a
nonpolitical group when he made a speech at the formal
opening of the Chinese Association's new building early in
January 1907, a gala occasion graced by the Japanese Imperial Band. "According to an old adage of our country," Wang
told the audience of over a thousand students, "the old men
are considered to be the pillars of a nation." Through contact
with Western nations, however, China had found that the
secret of success was wisely directed energy. Young people
were best able to push. It was their energy which, if wisely
directed, would better the world. "Among all the Chinese
young men, where do we find those possessing the greatest
amount of energy? You will readily agree with me that it is in
Japan." [92]

These oblique remarks could not be considered exactly revolutionary. Indeed, Wang did not want them to appear so, for
he was considering acceptance of an imperial scholarship for

study in the United States. At the same time, they were not antirevolutionary either, and the Association was not behaving in an antirevolutionary manner. In the reading room were copies of *Min Pao,* which the imperial Chinese government, with good cause, considered seditious.[93] Day after day students in Association rooms talked rebellion, and despite the bland neutrality of official Association policy, the Tokyo secretaries closed their eyes to the swirl of revolutionary activity in their building. Their reasoning was sound: they knew that if they were to strengthen the Association's bonds with students, they must provide a meeting place where education, tea, and open discussion would all be available. Clinton wrote, "We are at the fountain of China's new life." [94] They were indeed: one secretary stated flatly in 1911 that C. T. Wang, another Chinese secretary, and a good many of the Association members were also of the "society," by which he clearly meant the T'ung-meng hui.[95] In 1913 Sun Yat-sen, who had been in Japan throughout 1906 and in all probability knew some of the Western secretaries at that time, was introduced to an Association audience as an old and valued friend.[96] This is not to intimate that the Association itself was revolutionary, but to show that it would have friends if the revolution succeeded.

To some Westerners on the mainland, the Tokyo Association's permissiveness spelled suicide. In the middle of 1907 Logan Roots, a bishop of the Methodist Episcopal Church highly sympathetic to Association aims, protested vigorously about the availability of *Min Pao* in Tokyo, which he declared was seditious. It was already embarrassing enough that Sun Yat-sen was a Christian. "I feel very strongly," he wrote, "that it be made absolutely and consistently clear that the Church cannot be implicated with any political party whatever . . . thus obeying the injunction of our Savior 'Render unto Caesar the things that are Caesar's.' " [97] From China Willard Lyon assured Roots that the Tokyo headquarters had already circulated a statement to students making clear its nonpolitical nature. "We are not a political organization and can have nothing whatever to do with political projects." [98] That the statement should have been necessary indicates the extent of the revolutionary activity. Nevertheless, *Min Pao* remained in the reading room, students eagerly read a series of articles on the French revolution, and through the Association rooms went the cry that China could be purified only by a baptism of blood.[99]

The significance of the Tokyo Association's attitude cannot be overstressed, for by their actions the secretaries were forging an alliance with students from all over China. By responding to student needs at many levels, they established the Association as being truly sensitive to modern currents among the young. As these students swarmed back to China, they bore with them affection and respect for the Association. As the fortunes of the imperial government dimmed and the revolution approached, the Chinese Y.M.C.A. found itself, to quote Fletcher Brockman, "in touch with the highest aspirations of young China." [100] This most felicitous friendship, added to those of businessmen and officials, enabled the Association to prosper and grow in the following years.

Other opportunities for growth began to emerge on the mainland. After 1907 the Chinese Association experienced a boom as increased support in the United States and China made expansion a matter of planning rather than of dreaming. The reputation built so carefully began to return dividends in the shape of more staff, more members, more associations, and more backers. All these factors helped to extend to additional urban areas the services that had been tested on a small scale.

One sensitive indicator of growth was the number of Western personnel employed. By 1907 the Chinese Association had twenty-eight Western secretaries; five years later the number had tripled. This expansion in Western personnel reflected greatly increased backing by Westerners in both China and the United States. By 1907 the missionary community was well aware of the Association's power to reach young people, especially those of the upper classes. Although many of the more conservative ministers considered the Association's religious attitudes far too liberal, the China Centenary Conference of 1907, despite some grumbling, passed a series of resolutions praising the Association and recommending its expansion. With such high praise to back him up, John Mott was able to allocate funds for sending more secretaries to China. Further help appeared in 1908 when John D. Rockefeller, Jr., sent Ernest Burton of the University of Chicago to China at the request of the Centenary Conference to study educational problems. On his return, Burton lavished praise on Brockman and the Association's work in a lengthy report. Subsequently the report and Burton's good offices played a key role in securing for the Chinese Association a half-million dollars for new buildings, donated by Rockefeller and other wealthy Americans.[101]

The increase in Chinese personnel was even greater, as the Association vigorously pursued its attempt to find Chinese leaders. This policy was not mere window-dressing, for at the March 1907 Annual Convention, John Mott and Richard B. Morse, head of the American International Committee, were the only Western platform speakers.[102] Moreover, Willard Lyon started a small training school for secretaries in Shanghai. Regrettably, a complete list of Chinese personnel in these years has not come to light, but Lyon's list of the seven men being trained in Shanghai in 1910 is illuminating:

> Y. K. Fong, 22, son of a Shanghai merchant, baptized after he joined the Association.
>
> Lee Chung Fau, 28, son of a Foochow businessman, converted at the age of 16, graduate of the Anglo-Chinese college (presumably in Foochow).
>
> Tsang Tien-tsang, 20, born in Shaoshing, graduate of a Hangchow school, son of a Presbyterian pastor.
>
> Shih Pao Kwang, 22, son of a Tientsin merchant, graduated from Gailey's P'u T'ung School, converted by Y.M.C.A.
>
> Chen Hsueh Ching, 21, born near Peking, son of a pastor, graduate of P'u T'ung School.
>
> B. W. Zia, born near Hangchow, graduate of Hangchow College, training for physical directorship.
>
> Hoh Chwen Guan, 22, son of a military officer, mother a Christian, graduate of Union Christian College at Nanking.[103]

The Association evidently recruited its secretaries both from mission schools and from its own school, from Christian and from non-Christian families. Although the list does not show the occupations of secretaries before they entered Association employment, a later list reveals that over half the Chinese secretaries were recruited from among students and teachers.[104] Such men swelled the ranks of Chinese personnel from a total of sixteen in 1907 to over sixty by the revolution. They played an increasingly important part in the Association, as teachers, athletic instructors, editors, and administrators, besides performing the basic clerical and submanagerial functions of running an office.

The expansion in the Chinese staff reflected not only a modest rise in Association memberships, reaching about three thousand in these years, but also an increase in donations locally by Chinese friends. Building site funds further marked the interest and generosity of Chinese donors. Here, for example, are some of the Chinese donors to the fund to acquire land for a Peking Y.M.C.A. building:

Jeme (Chan) T'ien Yu (Yung Wing boy, chief engineer, Peking–Kalgan Railway)

Chen Chao Chang (Governor of Kirin, 1906)

Dr. Y. K. Tsao (later president of Tsinghua U.)

Alfred Sze (later minister to the United States)

Na Tung (president of Board of Revenue)

T'ang Shao I (later Premier)

Chu Pao Fay (Yung Wing boy, Telegraph service)

Liang Shih I (Director of Railways, 1907)

M. T. Liang (Liang Ju-hao, Customs taotai, Tientsin 1907) [105]

In Tientsin, the list of contributors to Association drives included Yuan Shih-k'ai, Wu T'ing-fang, and an official listed as Ou Yang Hsiu Te, who was trying to buy up the streetcar system of Tientsin.[106]

With so solid a financial basis, the Chinese Association moved optimistically into new cities, bringing in outstanding men. With the organization of Princeton-in-Peking in 1906, Dwight Edwards and John Stewart Burgess arrived to reinforce Robert Gailey. In the same year Robert Service, a track star from the University of California, went to Chengtu to explore the possibilities for student work. An Association primarily serving the business community was organized in Foo-chow in 1907 and had over three hundred members by 1910; a Canton group organized in 1908 soon had almost four hundred members. In the Nanking Association a doctor named F. B. Whitmore carried on minor medical work and organized college preparatory classes from about 1906, and Eugene Barnett arrived early in 1911 to start an Association in Hangchow. By 1911 Hugh Moran had begun an Association in Wuchang. Though statistics and records for these years are baffling and contradictory, they indicate that either Western personnel or untrained Chinese secretaries were exploring the possibilities of forming Associations in other cities, including Hinghwa (near Shanghai), Chefoo, and Tsingtao.[107]

Clearly the natural constituency for the Association in these years was the progressive element in the community, made up of persons who were interested in innovation both political and social. After the empress dowager died and as the imperial government became daily more corrupt and inept, the general desire for reform grew continually stronger, nourishing new Associations. Returned students cheated of a role in society could use the Association as a gathering place; businessmen increasingly contemptuous of a sagging central government could become leaders of change with the Association as part-ner. Against such a background, the familiar Y.M.C.A. services spread, throve, and added to the sum of social change in several cities.

Although each Association early developed a distinctive re-sponse to local needs, secretaries between 1907 and 1911 tried wherever possible to carry on vocational education, athletic programs, recreational services, and religious work, for which they found a good response. The services by then familiar to Shanghai and Tientsin were welcomed elsewhere, and the spread of this work constituted an indispensable part of modernization. All was not repetition of proven services, however, and several secretaries were able to introduce innovations, the more important being in Shanghai, Nanking, Chengtu, Tientsin, and Peking.

Shanghai, the national headquarters and home of the National Committee since 1896, boasted over a thousand members in its city Association by 1910. In addition to educational work, the Shanghai Y.M.C.A. published a thriving journal called *China's Young Men* or *Chung-kuo Ch'ing-nien,* written in easy wen-li or classical style and edited by H. L. Zia.[108] An athletic specialist named Max Exner had been brought to the city by the Association in 1908 to train Chinese physical directors and to develop an athletic program. The Association moved aggressively into community work as well. In 1909 it played a vigorous role in closing the opium shops in the city, and a former secretary, Tong Kai-son, became secretary to the International Opium Commission.[109] In addition, in 1907 the Shanghai Association shared in the general missionary program for the International Famine Relief fund, set up to aid famine victims in China.[110]

Nanking, which did not have a formal organization, became notable for athletics. In 1910 the merchants of the area, in response to prodding by Viceroy Tuan-fang, launched China's first large-scale industrial exposition. To ensure entertainment and adequate publicity, they asked the national Y.M.C.A. to organize an athletic meet. By that date athletics were thriving elsewhere; the Sixth Annual Meet in Tientsin, for example, had attracted seven thousand spectators. Accordingly Max Exner, the national physical director, organized a meet for the third week of October, drawing upon students from both north and south China. There was lively interest and high attend-

114

ance, with audiences ranging from an estimated ten thousand the first day to almost double by the end of the meet. Indicating the genuine popularity of such a spectacle were the facts that both Chang Po-ling and the viceroy appeared, Christian and government colleges participated formally, and the schools of Nanking were given a holiday.[111] This demonstration of modernity would have been unthinkable ten years before, and the excitement of the meet considerably enhanced the Association reputation.

In Chengtu, where athletics were also proving a point of contact with students, the new Association was experimenting with science. After Robert Service went to Chengtu in 1906, an English doctor named Henry Hodgkin joined him. Hodgkin carried on minor medical work and lectured on science and other subjects to government school students and teachers. Service, besides offering an athletic program, waged a determined campaign to make friends with the gentry.[112] In 1909 they were joined by another Englishman named William Wilson. Originally a medical evangelist in Suitingfu, Wilson had since become a science teacher. At Chengtu he built a science museum and prepared a formal science curriculum for students.[113] The Chengtu work was interesting not only because it duplicated the Tientsin work to some extent but also because it proved enormously popular in reform-minded Szechwan. When the provincial assembly first met, Chinese and Western Association personnel received a special invitation to attend, an honor accorded to no other foreigners in Chengtu.[114]

Of all the Association work in the two or three years before the revolution, however, two accomplishments have prime importance: the introduction of modern communication techniques through the lectures of C. H. Robertson, and the modest initiation of social work by Chinese students, first in Tientsin and then in Peking. Although full realization of the potential value of these two steps did not come until after the Revolution, the first efforts were made as far back as 1909.

By that year, C. H. Robertson had expanded his lecture series well beyond the field of science. In Paotingfu he gave an illustrated talk on government education in Chihli to more than a thousand people; in Nanking the provincial colleges asked him to lecture on China and the Olympics.[115] The enthusiastic response in both places encouraged him to envision a national lecture bureau that would include a welfare and publicity department, and would send out trained speakers to discuss the great ideas of the West. He sent off long, enthusiastic letters to John Mott, suggesting that they show moving pictures on subjects such as the U.S. Congress or the British Parliament; lecture on patent medicine, tuberculosis, elimination of the plague, or alcoholism; set up athletic fields; and provide film projectors and films.[116] He asked for $47,500 to begin the work.[117] Although the general idea of widespread work dated as far back as Timothy Richard, Robertson's ambitious concepts were overwhelming for their time. Back in the United States on furlough, he found that there were not enough funds for so large a project, and with typical energy he began to barnstorm the American Associations trying to raise support. A New Jersey lady gave him five hundred dollars for China's first tuberculosis exhibit, to be used at the Nanking Industrial Exhibition; a doctor gave him pathological specimens; others contributed material on the bubonic plague. Robertson noted that by the time he returned to China, he hoped to have equipment for lectures on the wireless telegraph, telautograph, telogrophone, gyroscope, aeronautics, snow crystals, and astronomy, to mention only a few of his subjects. He emphasized that he would use motion pictures wherever possible.[118] To run his national lecture campaign, however, he was assured of only $15,000 for the next four years.[119]

Back in China, Robertson spent the rest of 1910 busily running a one-man operation. He visited Canton, Hong Kong, Amoy, Swatow, Foochow, Shanghai, Taiyuan, Hankow, and Kuling, sometimes giving three lectures a day. In Shanghai he played to full houses. In Taiyuan the governor sent his own carriage and a request for a command performance; in Foochow, Robertson gave a private demonstration for the richest man in town and extracted ten thousand dollars from him for the Association's yearly campaign. He x-rayed officials' hands, demonstrated gyroscopes, and threw boomerangs at Manchu generals. Everywhere he was a hit.[120] "The lectures must be capable of producing a profound impression," stated his annual report in 1910.[121] His greatest contribution was recognition of the power of showmanship and of modern visual techniques, in short, the power of dramatic communication. He made plans for an audio-visual department for the Association that would put these techniques to use in many ways.

While Robertson was thus forging a means of dramatizing China's problems and potentialities, a wholly different theme was emerging within the Chinese Association in the shape of student interest in social welfare. The first Association work of this kind dated as far back as 1897, when members of the student Association at St. John's College (Sheng Yüeh-han) in Shanghai reportedly started a small day-school for the poor.[122] Owing to a lack of systematic reporting from mission schools, it is not known whether the work was duplicated elsewhere. The next known development came from the student Association at the Nankai Middle School. In 1909 Fletcher Brockman reported that Chang Po-ling had taken the initiative in forming a "Social Club" for students, with Chang as president and

R. M. Hersey of the Tientsin Association as vice-president.[123] Sometime thereafter club members undertook a modest project for children, teaching them games and keeping them clean.[124] Subsequently a club member named Ling Pian went to Tsing Hua University in Peking, founded by American indemnity funds, where he duplicated the work done in Tientsin. This concern was a new one, for although there were a few custodial agencies in China to help children, women, and the aged, there was no real community welfare work of the kind familiar to the West. Families took care of their own, and private benevolent agencies existed in places, but student welfare work apparently did not exist before this time.[125] It soon became clear that Chinese students, who knew nothing of the poor and neglected, were profoundly stirred by their problems.

In Peking, too, the idea of student social work was beginning to take hold. The new Association was carrying on successful educational work, giving part-time classes for customs employees, and initiating plans for north China student conferences. A number of boys from the Peking Interpreters' College, who had been gathered together by the secretary John Stewart Burgess for a Bible class, quickly made known that they were bored and preferred to discuss China's practical social needs. Burgess decided to meet their request. The Association must shift its focus in student work, he believed. Although it should not lose its original aim of demonstrating how Christianity could help China, it should turn to studying social, political, and economic questions on a systematic basis. In addition, the Association should initiate organized poor relief.[126] Thus quietly began what was to be an important element in Peking's future work.

These new themes, which were only minor strains in the over-all Association operation, went unnoticed among the events of 1910 and 1911. Political matters occupied the thoughts of most Chinese, for Szechwan was defying the imperial government, Tientsin students were rioting in the streets, Wu T'ing-fang had led a queue-cutting demonstration in Shanghai, and the end of the dynasty seemed imminent. Shortly before the imperial edifice crumbled, Brockman wrote, "The hitherto triumphant and almost hilarious march of progress and reform shows this year a sudden and ominous pause." [127] When the end came, Associations in southern cities were for a while more worried than pleased, leaving dates off their publications until they could tell which regime to date by, and watching financial campaigns waver in the general climate of uncertainty. But reassurance came rapidly. The outlook for the Chinese Association was glowing, wrote C. T. Wang to John Mott, because many of the revolutionary leaders were Christians, and the new government promised to be extremely tolerant in religious matters. Wang added, "It will be very easy now for us to get money for the Y.M.C.A. because the heads of departments are now our friends and school mates, to whom we can go at any moment." [128]

It was sixteen years since Willard Lyon had made his way reluctantly to Tientsin, turning his back on the traditional students in Peking. Lyon, Brockman, Gailey, Robertson, and others had pinned their faith on the certain emergence of a modern China, and they had courted the young Chinese who would bring that China into being. With the coming of the revolution, their faith seemed justified. They had caught the imagination of the new generation, and ahead lay untold opportunities for the Association and for China herself. The immediate task was to meet the challenge.

5

THE Y.M.C.A. AND COMMUNITY ACTION

The Association's initial exuberance was not wholly unjusti-
fied, for it was able to play an important role in the early
republican era. Despite the rapid discrediting of liberal political institutions, the period between 1911 and 1925 represented
a high point for moderate Sino-American organizations. During that time there was reasonable agreement between China's
self-diagnosis and Western prescriptions, and although the
American vision of a modern society did not suit Chinese
problems as closely as its advocates had hoped, it fit well
enough to leave a distinctive imprint.

The social reforms in China during the ten years following
the end of Ch'ing dynastic rule were primarily guided by
forces of the rising urban middle class: businessmen, officials,
educators, and the students who were their children. This
class included the modern professional man as well as the
urban rentier, a shifting group not easily defined in statistical
terms but generally characterized by some degree of education, property ownership, and patriotism. Despite the general
political chaos of the years after 1912, the urban middle class
prospered, for the times provided opportunities to acquire new
wealth and status. New light industries such as textiles, glass,
cement, and flour milling generated profits in Shanghai not
only for foreign investors but for Chinese as well; a heavy
industry complex in Wuchang produced a new group of industrialists and technical and managerial elites. Newspapers,
schools, and a growing film industry fed the public taste for
information and amusement. Businessmen who had begun to
achieve economic and political power in the turbulent times
before the revolution now successfully vied for social leader-

ship, a role increasingly vacated by the disintegrating gentry class. Into the great urban universities, now staffed by Chinese faculty and administrators, flowed the children of the middle class, for whom the expansion of China's economy promised prosperity and prestige. The optimism was founded in fact. To be sure, progress was neither universal nor uninterrupted, especially when political warfare and labor agitation became widespread in the twenties. But for a short space of years the new middle class found its personal aspirations reasonably well satisfied, and was able to look beyond them to the larger needs of China.

The model of progress, both individual and national, first adopted by the urban middle class was that of middle-class America. Many Chinese had been exposed to this model already as students in the United States, as businessmen in the mixed treaty-port society, or as students in mission schools. A substantial number were either Christian or sympathetic to Christianity. Thus, many of the treaty-port Chinese were partly familiar with American values and were willing to follow the advice of American reformers. These American reformers, who dispensed advice liberally in the newspapers, lectures, and face to face, were themselves usually products of a specific middle-class outlook born of a booming and mobile society. They had an implicit faith that self-reliance and self-improvement would generate personal opportunity, and that the private individual, in collaboration with like-minded men, could organize so as to raise the general level of social well-being. This faith in the potential of both the individual and society was now transmitted to China, where it held great appeal for the rising urban middle class.

As Chinese businessmen and educators became leaders in modernization, they found themselves in agreement with many American assumptions. The first point of agreement was acceptance of the primary importance of urban communities in a modern society. The entire story of the West, declared one young Chinese sociologist, was the history of its urban development. China's main hope seemed to lie in similar development—in the growth of urban industries, the spread of transportation facilities, the electrification of street lights, the growth of urban schools, the rise of a literate clerical and managerial class. The middle classes found it easy to adopt these Western values, for the same forces that promised to benefit China would also nourish them.

In designating those who would lead in the process of modernization, Western experience again nurtured middle-class ambitions, for it emphasized the role of elite groups as reformers. The American model of reform was the Progressive movement, which had made vigorous achievements on the urban level. The movement had been largely initiated by America's business-oriented middle class under the stimulus of the Social Gospel. The emphasis on elite leadership well suited the Chinese tradition that had long emphasized the role of the scholar-gentry, and which could now transfer this obligation to new elites. As direct heirs of the scholarly tradition, educators held a prominent position, but a major contender for leadership was the new and increasingly well-educated business class. As one businessman declared in a speech before the Chinese National Chamber of Commerce: "We know the conditions of our country and we know her needs and we can bring to her our experience and knowledge . . . Only the merchants, educationists, industrialists and bankers can have leisure and experience and can command the respect of the people." [1]

The Chinese middle class also emulated American reformers in espousing gradualism. It became quite clear in the months after the fall of the Ch'ing that merchants, to say nothing of the conservative provincial gentry, did not want social revolution. Moderate reform, not violent convulsion, met the requirements of the emerging Chinese power holders, who swiftly nudged the young revolutionaries from center stage. Merchants, finding ample economic opportunity, especially in the treaty ports, were reluctant to countenance changes that might undermine their prosperity or status. This partly reflected class timidity. The occasional clamor of new socialist movements grated on the sensibilities of a class that was testing its power and did not want to preside over its own demise. In addition, however, returned students from the United States could attest to the vigor of a country that insisted upon orderly private reforms. The distinguished educator Chang Po-ling summed up a popular point of view when he declared that China was too big to reform all at once. As he pointed out soon after the revolution: "The reform process is a good deal like trying to cook an immense lump of dough. If the fire is too hot, the outside is burned black and the inside is still raw." [2]

It would be easy to credit this belief in gradualism to a cynical self-interest. Yet it stemmed also from deep currents in American and Chinese thought. Basic to both traditions was a faith in the power of education to work miracles in transforming man and, through him, society at large. "The most urgent [problem] of all is the overcoming of ignorance," the scholar Yen Fu had written in analyzing China's weaknesses, "for our failure to cure poverty and weakness stems from our ignorance." [3] This belief, deeply ingrained by centuries of Chinese history, found an echo among reformers in the new era and provided them with a general blueprint. At the individual level, education in schools would provide the tools for self-improvement, so that eventually there would be enough educated individuals to strengthen China herself. The concept of education was comprehensive: it did not mean formal schooling alone, but a constellation of methods ranging from part-time schools and vocational institutions to public lectures on citizenship or sanitation. Insistence on individual effort in learning was the key. This value is implicit in any modern society, perhaps especially so in China and the United States. In China of the republican era, it represented not so much an evasion of larger issues as an optimism that education could work widely and quickly to solve a variety of problems. That such methods, commendable in themselves, could transform society only in combination with favorable economic and political environments was a fact that reformers did not always wholly comprehend.

Thus, the urban middle class expressed its hopes for reform in terms of moderate values. Education, health, self-improvement, thrift, and moral character were its watchwords, as reflected in the reforms it set in motion. To the efforts of the national and provincial governments it added its own. The years following the revolution saw a proliferation of schools, health societies, savings clubs, and children's playgrounds. If this were its entire achievement, the middle class would still have made a contribution to society during this era. But in addition, the American vision went beyond a hope of neat schoolhouses, solvent families, and children with clean teeth. Drawing from their own experience, American reformers also urged the Chinese middle class to consider the special problems arising from urbanization and industrialization.

Just as rapid urban growth in the West had created mass social evils, so was it creating a similar situation in China.

Opportunity in the cities and disturbances in the countryside caused by political warfare and famine were bringing huge numbers of unskilled rural workers into the city. Shanghai, for example, grew from under 1,000,000 people in 1900 to 1,600,000 in 1920. Many flowed into the new industries as a source of cheap labor, unprotected even by the paternalistic safeguards that characterized the premodern Chinese labor tradition. Men, women, and children as young as six years old worked sixteen hours a day, seven days a week, in dark lofts. The man who could not find employment in industry eked out a living as a rickshaw puller. Many of the unemployed poor became ash pickers, scavengers, or if the guild did not prevent them, beggars. One particularly miserable product of the times were the "gleaners," women who ran after the coolies unloading sugar at the docks, ready to sift out stray grains from the dirt underfoot.[4] In the sweatshops and crowded tenements, the illiteracy, disease, and poverty already present in Chinese cities assumed a new size and visibility. Humanitarian considerations pressed for a response, joined by the recognition that a new class ripe for militant appeals was being formed.

Western experience declared that China's search for wealth and power must incorporate a solution for these mass social evils. Women and children should be protected from exploitation, education made available, disease controlled, poverty alleviated by training. Here again the middle class was expected to take the lead. The failure of the Chinese urban middle class to accomplish this massive task has been insistently proclaimed. There is, however, another side to the chronicle. The middle class was not monolithic in its response, and many of its members did not reject the demands of serious social problems. There were plenty of individual heroes and heroines. The difficulty lay in their working within a demanding environment and being called upon for a type of activity with which they were not particularly familiar. It was not so easy to be a reformer in China as in the United States.

To begin with, the sheer size of social problems was much greater in China. Illiteracy was reckoned at from 80 to 90 percent. Even in enlightened and progressive Tientsin, only about 4 percent of the elementary-school-age children were estimated to be in school. Most primary school teachers, according to one sharp criticism, "had never entered a class room as students before they became teachers." [5] Health problems were equally large, with a high incidence of tuberculosis and intestinal infection. No one attempted to keep statistics on the number of people living below subsistence levels. These staggering problems were coupled with China's severely limited economic resources, most of which drained into support of armies and government administration. Private institutional funds were unable to meet the demand. [6]

A major problem, however, was that the Chinese middle class as a whole did not have the same tradition of response that existed in the United States. In America, social action was largely voluntary. Militant women's clubs and neighborhood organizations founded settlement houses, enlarged educational opportunities, and fought for the protection of workers. Although private groups urged the government to pass appropriate measures, the liberal faith of the era basically distrusted government intervention. It placed responsibility for originating and often financing reform upon private, voluntary groups, who became a powerful force before the era when the welfare state had been defined or established.

In the United States, there existed an ambiguous but undeniable community spirit that could generate community action. Community spirit can be defined as a willingness to help people who do not necessarily have close ties or shared values springing from family, church, and class similarities or from geographical proximity. In the United States the wellsprings of this concern were both pragmatic and religious. At the level of practical self-interest, the sense of community meant the ability to see human beings in cities as experiencing a new interdependence, in which an individual's well-being was affected by the well-being of others. At the outermost limit, it meant concern for others simply because they were human beings, a conviction implicit in the universalistic Christian tradition. Neither then nor later did these beliefs reign supreme in the United States, but the sense of responsibility toward others was pervasive enough in the American middle class to give strength to the impulse toward voluntary community service. Aided by the American talent for organization, middle class leaders planned reforms and mobilized public opinion, volunteer workers canvassed club members and neighbors, and a large number of sympathetic people were moved to give money, perform services, or vote at the polls. Thus, the energy of a small but active group often acted as a catalyst to generate wide community response.

Chinese observers of the West viewed this phenomenon enviously, for it had no counterpart in China. To Yen Fu, the miracle of the West lay in "its ability to promote the constructive self-interest of the individual." Western society was able to release individual energies, yet harness these energies to collective goals. As Benjamin Schwartz has observed, Yen could find no similar spirit in China, which at best harnessed the social sense of the individual to other individuals and to very small groups.[7] This sentiment was echoed later by John Burgess of the Y.M.C.A., who noted that the Peking guilds had no sense of community responsibility.[8]

China did have many voluntary groups who carried on philanthropic and educational work. The role of the family and clan as educator, philanthropist, and keeper of the peace has been documented at length. The role of the rural gentry in maintaining order, repairing dikes, and administering relief has also been adequately recorded. In the cities, too, private individuals and groups took upon themselves some social responsibilities. Each major city had a network of voluntary philanthropic institutions under the auspices of provincial clubs and trade or craft guilds.[9] The comprador guild carried on a relief program for its members.[10] Yet such efforts were generally limited to those close to the guilds themselves. Most major reforms in China had been left to the government. Historically there was a psychological barrier to widespread private action, particularly by a business class with traditionally low prestige. Yet in an era of rapidly changing, ineffective national governments and widely varying provincial governments, cooperation and innovation by private groups were imperative.

Since there was no free-floating "universal ethic" uniting disparate groups, even within the business class, an attempt to inspire community action faced problems. Such an attempt would have to start either by creating such an ethic or by finding wholly different sources from which social concern might come. The task required special leadership. Given the jealous provincialism and particularism endemic in the country, community action required a group that could override particular concerns and persuade different groups of the need for common action. An organization free of the suspicion of self-interest and trained in pooling the energies of the middle class could perform an important function. The Chinese Y.M.C.A. emerged in this role.

The Y.M.C.A. was suited by predilection, by public accept-ance, and by experience to become a prime mover in stimulat-ing the Chinese middle class to widespread community action. Western secretaries were deeply committed to service. One of the slogans of the Chinese Association was *ch'ün,* meaning "the social organism" or "community." Service was its primary reason for being in China, and it could not easily be accused of jealous self-interest. It steadily advanced Chinese secretaries into positions of major responsibility. Western secretaries also had considerable experience in organizing activities such as fund-raising campaigns, which brought businessmen, educa-tors, and officials together in a common cause. The Associa-tion's interests and actual organization were both local and national. It was identified with the middle class as a whole instead of with a single group: as one businessman told the secretary Eugene Barnett in Hangchow, the Association build-ing was the only place where all the guilds could meet on neutral ground.[11] The Y.M.C.A. had won thousands of friends in two decades of painstaking effort. Thus, the organization was in a unique position to bring together the scattered ener-gies of different groups within the middle class, and it had the vision to see that this might be done. In the decade following the revolution, the Association worked to uncover and coordi-nate bases for community action in Chinese society. Working through friends and members, it successfully involved many middle class Chinese in working for large community objec-tives, and its activities helped to increase the Chinese sense of participating in a wider community than the family or guild.

Despite the political chaos that engulfed China in the years after 1911, the Y.M.C.A. was able to carry on its work in a generally cordial atmosphere. The early hope for the ascend-ancy of political progressives committed to "the Christian concepts of liberty, equality, and fraternity" flickered out quickly.[12] The brief Nanking government of returned students and Christians dissolved. In the provinces young returned students were pushed into retirement, and from Tientsin came the sad report that reactionaries were obstructing progress.[13] Despite the Association's sympathies for the progressives around Sun Yat-sen, however, it also had friends and supporters in the power elite that emerged around Yuan Shih-k'ai. The coalition cabinet announced in March 1912 included many old friends, members, and backers of the Association, including Ts'ai Yuan-p'ei, Wang Ch'ung-hui, C. T. Wang, Liang Tun-yen, and T'ang Shao-yi as premier. Most important, Yuan himself had long been sympathetic to the Association program of moderate reform. Through the political storms of the following years, therefore, the Association steered a generally safe course until the nationalist hysteria of 1925.[14]

As the new republic was getting underway, the Association held a meeting in Shanghai in May 1912 to determine what direction the organization should take. Secretaries had justifiable cause for optimism, for in recent months money from the United States and from Chinese sources had made rapid expansion possible. There were now 75 Western secretaries and 85 Chinese secretaries serving 25 city Associations and 105 student Associations. Eight new buildings had been erected; money for eight more was formally pledged. Associations claimed almost ten thousand members. A solid base thus existed for expansion.

There was no question about the general theme of Association work for the years ahead. As always, it was to be service, and service to more people than ever before. The Chinese Association, declared Fletcher Brockman, must take into account all young men—the urban middle class, railroad employees, working men, soldiers, sailors, policemen, streetcar operators, rickshaw men, even young men in rural areas. Its concerns were even larger, for plans were already underway to start working with younger boys, and the specter of the poor, both young and old, men and women, had long since touched the emotions of Association workers. To expand services was imperative; the question was how much, how fast, and in which directions. Although the industrial field, for example, required help in such areas as technical training or educational programs, the Association veered off from the problem, since it had no experience with industrial workers, no special funds for experimentation, and a vague hint that Catholic missionaries had undergone "a bad experience" with guilds.[15] Rural work was out of the question, as there was more than enough to do in the cities. The overwhelming needs of the poor demanded drastic solutions, which Brockman knew in the end only Chinese society itself could provide, rather than any single organization with limited resources. Essentially, students and middle class businessmen must remain the focus of Association concern, for students were still the organization's basic target, and businessmen its largest source of funds.

Assessing resources against needs, therefore, the secretaries made several significant decisions. They would continue their customary services for business people and students through general and vocational education, athletics, recreation, and publications. Religious education was to continue in the usual moderate vein, despite growing missionary complaints that Y.M.C.A. religious work secretaries were too liberal and that "a sermon given in the 'Y' is not a sermon." [16] These programs, already demonstrated to be useful and popular, would constitute the core of Association work. In addition, the Association would use such remaining resources and ingenuity as it possessed to serve other needs in the community.

With immediate objectives thus delineated, the Association set out to serve the new republic. It continued to open schools and build dormitories, gymnasia, and swimming pools. It taught English and business subjects in day schools, night schools, and even in "Hour-A-Day Schools." [17] A press bureau published quantities of self-help literature, and as early as 1913 the Association began to use the vernacular in printed materials.[18] By then the organization was only one of many carrying on educational work, but in athletics it remained pre-eminent for a time. With the help of Association traning, Chinese athletes took second place at the first Far Eastern Games, held in Manila in May 1913, and took first place in the second series, held in Shanghai in May 1915.[19] These athletic triumphs not only nourished the spirit of Chinese nationalism but also made new friends for the Association. The Association cooperated with other Western and Chinese organizations in the International Famine Relief Program. To emphasize the Association's close identification with China, C. T. Wang became the first Chinese general secretary in 1915, assuming top responsibility for the Chinese Y.M.C.A.

Yet the Association could not ignore the pressing larger social problems around it, and decided to tackle some of these with such weapons as it had at hand. The major weapon was the lecture program being carried on by C. H. Robertson. Robertson's lectures had been changing from an emphasis exclusively on science to a broader concern with other aspects of modern life. Even in the middle of the revolution, the response of Chinese leaders to his programs on athletics, physical fitness, and science had been enthusiastic. The Association therefore planned to set up a lecture bureau staffed by professionals in a number of fields. This bureau would attempt to spread information about modern life to leaders throughout the country, who might then take over the task of initiating reforms.

Moreover, the Association decided to encourage students to meet some of the needs that the organization alone could not tackle. This decision was born as much of desperation as of vision. Students were still the Association's primary concern, yet keeping their friendship and commitment was not a simple affair. The Association could not hope to provide an ostentatious program, for the hard fact was that Chinese merchants, the financial bulwark of the Y.M.C.A., were not interested in spending their money on Chinese students, and student work itself brought in no money. Nor did study groups devoted to religious questions have any appeal, since personal salvation rarely concerned Chinese students. Nevertheless, students could not be ignored, for already other organizations were vying for their attention, including a new socialist club in Peking. Several Associations reported a possible line of action. As students wanted to be active and constructive, and were already interested in social service, such service by students themselves might have a modest value in engaging their imagination. Secretaries therefore agreed to encourage students to study Western sociology, start voluntary night schools, and even give lectures on reform patterned after those of the lecture bureau. At the very least, such work would give students a sense of participation and usefulness.[20]

These decisions were underlying factors in the reforms of the decade after the revolution. The familiar Association services, intrinsically valuable because they served young middle class men in constructive ways and helped to diffuse modern living further through urban society, helped to strengthen and extend the network of influence that could make other Y.M.C.A. work acceptable to the Chinese public. The middle class alliance was indispensable to the type of work the Association hoped to do. Use of the lecture system offered a dramatic technique to attract attention, and enlisting of students in social service supplied the workers. All these factors worked as a leaven in Chinese social reform.

Most studies of Chinese students have concentrated on their behavior beginning with the May Fourth period of 1919. Because of this chronological concentration, little attention has been paid to student concerns in an earlier era, particularly before 1915. It is clear that even in this earlier period, students in many cities were developing an active interest in the poor, which certainly was the genesis of social concern during the May Fourth era. Part of this interest developed from the Y.M.C.A. enlistment of students in social service work.

After the secretarial planning meeting of May 1912, John Stewart Burgess of Peking set about to expand the modest social welfare work that Peking students were carrying on under Association auspices. In October 1912, he arranged for a conference of government school students at Robert Gailey's summer home in Wo Fo-ssu. The conference stressed the theme of social work and presented lectures entitled "The Relation of the Study of Sociology to Social Reform" and "The Problems of a Chinese City—What Chinese Students Can Do To Solve These Problems." [21] Consequently, student delegates decided to form a social service league. The day after the conference, thirty students from six Peking colleges met at Gailey's house and formed the Pei-ching She-hui Shih-chin hui or Peking Students' Social Service Club. [22]

As Burgess cast about for work that the club might do, he

learned that students were deeply interested in the social conditions of the poor but knew nothing about them.[23] He therefore arranged to have members conduct an informal social survey of rickshaw coolies. Early in November 1912, the club held what Burgess thought was probably the first "social clinic" in China. Several of the club members went into the street and persuaded a number of coolies to enter the building where the clinic was taking place. Once each man was inside the door, a panel of students asked him a battery of seventy-five questions on health, recreation, education, religion, and the history of China, after which he was rewarded with a bag of millet.[24]

The experience must have been extraordinary for the coolies. It was a revelation to the students and to Burgess himself, for previously they had known little about the quality of life among China's poor. "What . . . are we to preach to this poor, half-starved, ignorant coolie struggling for existence?" asked Burgess. "What message can you give him but food and clothing and a minimum of comfort?" Notions of reaching simple solutions began to disappear. The club, its members decided, needed to educate itself for a practical approach to service, which meant discovering the real needs of the poor. Having talked to thirty coolies, the students decided to interview a thousand and then plan for their relief.[25] This approach later led to a larger survey of rickshaw men, to studies of Peking industry, and to landmark studies of city and country by such men as John Burgess and secretary Sidney Gamble.

While club members were thus engaged in social investigation, the general student population in Peking was being swept up by a wave of enthusiasm for reform. In November, two college professors and a Y.M.C.A. secretary from the United States lectured in Peking on social work engaged in by students in America. Their lectures brought out a thousand government school students and an even larger number of mission school students.[26] In February 1913, Charles Henderson of the University of Chicago lectured on student responsibility for the lower classes of society.[27] In the fall, the Association itself presented a series of lectures. Their titles are instructive, for they indicate the growing scope of Association interest and its hopes for student participation: "The Need for Chinese Students To Enter into Social Service," "Moral Problems in China," "Social Service in American and British Universities," "The Social Settlement" (that is, the settlement house), "The Cause of Poverty," "The Value of Public Opinion and How To Arouse It," and "The Wider Significance of Social Service." [28]

Under such stimuli, club membership increased, and club members began extensive social service work in the community. They opened two model playgrounds for Peking children and gave a dinner for coolies to demonstrate their concern for the poor. They undertook an open-air lecture campaign and spoke on patriotism, science, reform, and hygiene, using lantern slides and handbills printed by themselves in the vernacular.[29] At Tsing Hua University, student Y.M.C.A. members started two part-time schools.[30] In August 1913, the club led twelve students from North China Union College and Union Medical College, both missionary institutions, to make the first serious study of social service institutions ever carried out in Peking.[31] The novelty and usefulness of such activity attracted others. By early 1915, club membership had climbed to six hundred, most of the members being students from government schools. The new president, Hsu Pao-ch'ien, had become a Y.M.C.A. secretary.[32] "The club has become the one great organizing force for social work among the 8,000 college men of the city," wrote John Burgess.[33] This by no means implied that the club was alone in carrying on humanitarian work. Its investigations in Peking had turned up one fine Buddhist orphanage and two others not so fine, a number of popular education movements, a model industrial school for boys, a "good many" free private schools, and eleven street lecture halls modeled after the Christian street chapels and devoted primarily to talks on Chinese history and philosophy.[34] It was the club organized by the Association, however, that attracted students.

Elsewhere in China, similar patterns were developing. At Soochow University (Tung-wu Ta-hsüeh), twenty-three students started a free tuition school for poor boys. At St. John's University in Shanghai, where a free school begun in 1897 was operating successfully, students had not only established an elementary school by 1914 but also provided a scholarship for a poor student from their own funds. St. John's students even extended their activities outside the city to staff a day school in a neighboring village. The Foochow Y.M.C.A. day school students managed a day and night school for poor boys; the Canton Y.M.C.A. ran a school for a hundred poor boys; the Tientsin Association was attempting an ambitious program of popular education, with students from five government schools giving lectures on health at church street chapels in the city. From city after city, Y.M.C.A. secretaries reported active participation by their student members in social service work.[35]

Such a burst of social concern was significant in many ways. The concern itself was meaningful, for it preceded the slow crumbling of barriers between the student elite and China's lower classes. The work was one assertion of student initiative and leadership beginning to emerge in China's changing society. The humanitarian program as such could not fail to do good. Most important, the tendrils of social responsibility were beginning to penetrate to the students, as the Association had hoped they might. Students in a number of cities were now infected with enthusiasm for social service, and by example and exhortation they might in turn infect others.

The small but undoubted success of the social service movement prompted Association secretaries to expand and guide the movement more efficiently. In 1914, John Burgess sounded the theme that would characterize the years ahead. In an article written for *The Chinese Recorder* he defined social service as being everything that men did to accomplish the purpose of God the world over. The greatest work that could be done in China at the time was social and moral reform, especially in the form of service to the lower classes, but philanthropic societies, for all their usefulness, were limited in value. To be truly effective, reform demanded large solutions created by a wave of public opinion. The task ahead was to mobilize the public.[36]

Already the Association was attempting to use students as agents in this public mobilization, not only by giving them on-the-spot guidance wherever possible, but also by instructing them in print on the specifics of shaping public opinion. Roscoe Hersey, a Tientsin secretary (and father of the later American novelist), produced a manual entitled *Social Service* introducing students to the possibilities in the area and telling them how to go about it. "The consciousness of interdependence," wrote Hersey, "will develop with the advance of modern civilization. The development of great industries and the centralizing of plants will bring new social helpfulness. Because of this and other similar forces which are at work, it is highly important that every possible effort now be made to develop a spirit of community sympathy. We should seek out those activities and promulgate those ideas which will tend to lead the community to brotherhood and democracy." [37]

Many students, Hersey noted, were already at work establishing schools and serving as volunteer teachers, and education in schools was certainly integral to China's progress. There were, however, other ways to educate the rising generation. In the West, various methods of popular education were now being carried on, particularly through a widespread system of popular lectures. In China this new lecture technique might be extremely important in awakening the community: "We live in a period of transition and change and an important aim should be to develop a social consciousness. This is a fundamental task, for the success of all social welfare movements depends upon securing a social consciousness of the need of change . . . It is necessary that questions relating to public welfare should be discussed and made public." [38]

Such efforts, Hersey continued, were an easy form of service for students, which many were already performing. New and dramatic adjuncts to straight lectures were also available. The stereopticon was being used in most mission colleges and many government institutions. The new lecture department of the Association had a slide exchange available to students through their schools. "Lantern lectures, especially where accompanied by music, prove powerful instruments for educating those of the masses who are not willing to attend night schools," the pamphlet stated.[39] All these techniques could help to spread knowledge of the modern world.

To this analysis the pamphlet added an emphatic reminder that proper planning and organization were imperative. A successful school demanded a modest start, reliable teachers, and students whose parents would ensure their attendance. In public education, good planning and organization were even more important, for a citywide campaign demanded the utmost care in development and execution. What the Association meant by careful organization, Hersey explained at length. The Tientsin Association, for example, had prepared 50,000 welfare calendars in colloquial Chinese for distribution throughout the city. Students from twenty-one schools and colleges then met to make plans for distributing the calendars. A map of the city was cut into sections, and the representative from each institution took a piece of the map back to his school. In some cases the maps were enlarged so that the exact location of each street and alley could be seen. Then the students were divided into bands of four, each band taking a definite street or neighborhood. The three hundred and eighty-five students taking part in this campaign efficiently spread the calendars throughout Tientsin. Some months later the same student bodies united to distribute 100,000 leaflets setting forth the dangers of flies, mosquitoes, and rats, using the same distribution technique except that the leaflets were also given out in teahouses, shops, and on the streets.[40] Similarly well-organized campaigns were being duplicated to a lesser degree in other cities.

Accustomed as we are today to high pressure canvassers and campaigners, the instructions in Hersey's pamphlet seem obvious. In China in 1914, however, they represented orderly and rather sophisticated methods of social persuasion. The use of enthusiastic volunteers, modern communication techniques, and careful organization provided the ingredients for what today would be called a mass propaganda effort. One factor still missing was size, but it could be supplied merely by adding campaigns and involving more people. The other missing factor was more subtle, for it involved the psychological element in propaganda. A successful campaign needed to employ symbols that would arouse the emotions of the Chinese at their most sensitive places. The Y.M.C.A. professional lecture bureau was learning the nature of those symbols, and was thereby refining techniques for moving the Chinese community to action.

While the bustle of Association activity was increasing, C. H. Robertson continued his own vivid lectures on science and religion. His faith in the power of lectures to mold the opinion of China's leaders infected many of those who saw him in action, and the potential of mass lectures in covering other subjects became clear. Soon after the revolution, a group of returned students approached Fletcher Brockman with the suggestion that the Y.M.C.A. begin interpreting to the leaders of the nation "the deeper meaning of modern civilization." [41] Accordingly, a lecture bureau was formally organized by the National Committee in 1912, and David Yui (Yü Jih-chang), a journalist and educator, left the editorial staff of the *Peking Daily News* to become its secretary. Brockman made plans for the bureau's expansion.

Chinese leaders were most interested in lectures on the need for education. Yuan Shih-k'ai tentatively promised financial aid if the lecture bureau would set up a training program for government lectures on education. Robertson cooperated with the new Chinese National Education Association in organizing a lecture training staff to operate throughout the country; the commissioner of education for Kwangtung Province drew up a plan for a provincial lecture series, and the National Board of Education announced a national lecture system. [42]

The campaign for schools was not, however, the first social problem tackled by the lecture bureau. As Robertson himself was not an education expert, one would have to be procured if the lectures were to become professional. For the moment, therefore, the Association decided to leave the problem of combating illiteracy to its volunteer student-teachers. In the bureau itself, Brockman first coped with a problem that in the United States had been especially amenable to public education, namely, public health.

To catalog the medical and health needs of China would be to write volumes on disease and suffering. Tuberculosis was chronic. Cholera raged year after year. In 1911 a pneumonic plague epidemic developed. Both missionaries and Chinese doctors (notably Wu Lien-te) carried on curative work, but as far as the medical world knew, no large-scale preventive measures had ever been attempted in the country.[43] China had no vital statistics, no quarantine laws except in ports under maritime customs, no boards of health laws, and no cooperative effort to avoid disease. The China Medical Missionary Association had spoken of starting mass work, but as of 1912 nothing had been done.

By the time of the revolution, the Y.M.C.A. had begun to experiment in public health, having printed a book on tuberculosis and made it available to doctors at cost. The booklet immediately went into three editions, and the Association relinquished publication rights so that anyone could print it.[44] Knowledge of the book and of Robertson's effective lectures encouraged the China Medical Missionary Association to request that the Y.M.C.A. begin a program of popular education on behalf of public health. By early 1912 Brockman had found a suitable doctor to head the work, a new arrival in China named William Wesley Peter.

Dr. Peter had gone to China with his bride, who was also a doctor, just before the October 1911 hostilities. He immediately reported to the Red Cross in Hankow and was assigned to tend wounded soldiers in Li Yüan-hung's army until such time as he might be released for work in Hunan as a medical missionary. Early in 1912, however, Fletcher Brockman wrote to suggest that Peter join the Lecture Bureau to work on public health. Peter responded enthusiastically. There was much work to do, he wrote, not only curative but preventive, and the tools were apparently at hand to make such work possible. Peter, who was an amateur photographer with a keen eye, had already seen and been profoundly impressed by Robertson's dramatic demonstrations. His lantern slides and other visual aids offered new possibilities in public health education. The Association would have to lead the way, however, since the task was too big for any one church. If the program were run properly, it might ultimately sow a seed in China, which the Chinese might continue to cultivate themselves. "Some of the student class too might thus be led to realize the importance of national health," he added, "and after securing adequate medical training, return to lead their own people." [45]

In 1913 the missionary group sponsoring Dr. Peter released him to the Association.[46] Robertson had already established a small laboratory in Shanghai, where Chinese assistants built and repaired scientific apparatus and produced visual aids. There Peter planned a series of popular and dramatic lectures on health. At the same time, he cooperated with Secretary Eugene Barnett and the Hangchow Y.M.C.A. in a small-scale public health campaign in that city. The Association had bought twenty thousand antituberculosis calendars, which the commissioner of police, one of Barnett's cooperative friends, sent his men to distribute to food sellers and to the general public.[47] Early in 1914 the Health Division became an official part of the national lecture bureau.

The work contemplated for the new Health Division was

outlined by Fletcher Brockman in a long report in the middle of 1914. Although the division reflected a direct outgrowth from Robertson's work, it had significant additions. Dr. Peter would head a staff of experts in health and in visual education. While Dr. Peter himself prepared and delivered lively popular lectures on health, his staff would prepare other lectures that doctors and laymen might give. They planned to use the Robertson technique of focusing on leaders, wrote Brockman, but added a step. They would start with leaders, but only in order to work through them to reach the common people, who were the real objective in public health. To achieve so ambitious a goal, the program would go beyond lecturing to include actual health campaigns. For these, Peter planned to use both persuasive visual aids and efficient community organization. A press bureau would popularize the health work through cartoons, popular literature, slides, films, and exhibits. A network of local doctors and leaders, organized and assisted by local Associations, would serve as a nucleus in each city. If all went well, local and even national health leagues would be formed.

Effective public health work by its very nature demanded widespread cooperation. To help the small professional health staff and the eventual health leagues, Brockman planned to enlist the entire community. With the aid of the Association's host of friends, the growing pool of student volunteers, and the new interest in preventing disease, he believed that Chinese communities might be induced to accept responsibility for their own health.[48]

Not only in W. W. Peter but also in the head of the new Visual Aids Division was the Association fortunate in its leadership. George Herbert Cole, formerly a science lecturer at McGill University in Toronto, was a gifted tinkerer like C. H.

Robertson. Cole had originally been expected to work with the Chinese upper classes in response to Timothy Richard's plea, but had finally been sent to Tokyo to help staff the Chinese Student Y.M.C.A. there. When he arrived in China to develop a visual program, he already had on hand a number of donated exhibits on miscellaneous subjects, ranging from science to health to sights in Western cities.[49] He immediately set to work to prepare more pertinent material. Cole operated on the assumption that exhibits attempting to touch the emotions of the Chinese should use symbols and slogans meaningful to them. This idea was not new, since the need for "Chineseness" had been recognized earlier by Matthew Ricci, Timothy Richard, and Robert Gailey. With Cole, however, the idea was translated into a new medium, for he sought out the sources of Chinese interest, pride, and concern susceptible to visual expression. From the new bureau flowed material that fed upon the Chinese love of color and drama, affection for children, subtlety of attitude toward life and death, and rising national pride. Incorporated into Peter's lectures, this material added a new and powerful dimension to the popular lectures that were beginning to indoctrinate the public.

The few original slides and many snapshots taken by Dr. Peter still in existence suggest the inventiveness of Cole's displays. They amuse and instruct. There were cartoons demonstrating elementary health rules for children, as well as a tuberculosis calendar built around Brother Fat and Brother Lean, with Brother Lean, who won out against disease by proper health habits, turning up fat and healthy at Brother Fat's funeral. A printed broadside featuring a huge fly next to a child announced, "If people don't kill flies, flies will kill people." There was a model of a Chinese house with a working door, out which a man walked every thirty-seven seconds and fell into a conveniently placed coffin, in a graphic illustration of China's death rate. There were gadgets with lights that flashed and dials that pointed, skulls labeled "death" that dropped from the ceiling, and six-foot cardboard flies. The exhibits made their point dramatically; as one elderly lady pointed out in a remark celebrated in Association annals, "If the flies are that big in America, no wonder they're afraid of them." [50]

Time and again, secretaries involved in the lecture work emphasized the importance of such lively visual materials in capturing Chinese interest and appealing to the Chinese humor. By 1915, Peter and the Association had produced a million Brother Fat and Brother Lean calendars, and with the cooperation of the newly organized National Health Council of the China Medical Missionary Association they were trying to have the calendars distributed by doctors at a cost of ten cash (copper coins) per calendar. Peter also used the material as the nucleus of an ambitious campaign involving all-day exhibits, meetings, lectures, and slide demonstrations. In January 1915, the first public health exhibit in China was held at the Medical Missionary conference in Shanghai, and soon thereafter campaigns were conducted in Changsha, Siangtan, and Nanking.[51]

Reinforcing the appeal of the visual exhibits was meticulous planning, which also reflected a knowledge of Chinese psychology. Campaigns were begun by enlisting the aid of leaders in the area under consideration. The influential people of a town, pointed out an Association manual entitled "How To Hold a Successful Health Campaign," must stand behind the program. It was especially advisable to place on the sponsoring committee not only the office-holders but also their potential successors, since one never knew what might happen in the middle of a campaign.[52] Fortunately, such backing was available because of the Association's large circle of well-wishers. Merchants, guilds, policemen, teachers, Taoist and Buddhist priests, and officials were included on its roster of friends. The Changsha chief of police initiated the request for a health exhibit himself and paid part of the expenses.[53] The wife of Feng Kuo-chang, later to become president of China, sponsored a campaign.[54] Social service clubs in Shanghai, Tientsin, Peking, Chuchow, and Chengtu began to emphasize public health. Thus, many influential groups could clearly be persuaded to band together for community welfare if proper advance planning was carried out. Leaders were no longer passive.

From the beginning, imagination and organization worked together. As the campaigns grew ambitious enough to attract large and varied audiences, who constituted that larger "community" whose interest Brockman intended to engage, it became necessary to advertise the exhibits more widely. Peter adopted a technique which he maintained was "a brand new stunt" in China. In 1911, Dr. O. T. Logan in Chengteh, Hunan, had hired coolies to march through the streets banging a gong to bring people to his hospital for treatment during an epidemic. Peter adapted the technique to a squad of sandwich-board men. On their backs and chests were signs that read

Health Exhibit
Health Meeting

Come to the Forbidden City
if you can get a ticket

Health
Have You Got It?
Has China Got It?

Come to the Meetings
with a proper ticket

In addition, the men often shouted out news of the exhibit
for the benefit of illiterates. The boxes containing the exhibit,
all painted black with the Y.M.C.A. red triangle on the side,
were carried through the streets by coolies, who improvised
songs about the exhibits as they went.[55]

Such methods attracted large audiences to the exhibits.
Inside the halls where the demonstrations were held, the same
careful planning had been at work. Audiences were divided by
status. People were moved from exhibit to exhibit and from
hall to hall to avoid boring them, and were served tea whenever possible. The lectures themselves were often dialogues
between Peter and the audience. For example, he would ask
what guaranteed national health, and the audience always
roared, "Money." The Association gave away door prizes, at
least once in the form of toy coffins, presumably to give a
sense of security to burial-conscious Chinese.[56] The campaigns
sound rather like an Oriental version of the old American
medicine show, and they were just as popular.

These health campaigns began to show visible proof of the
community spirit that the Association had hoped to evoke. In
Nanking, the Health Bureau held special meetings for women,
at which the governor's wife spoke. In Changsha, the chief of
police became first president of the new public health society,
and not long afterward a new tuberculosis hospital was
financed and built by public-spirited Chinese. Another public
health society was formed in Kaifeng. In Peking, the Ministry
of the Interior sponsored forty-six public health meetings.[57]
Both officials and local community leaders were beginning to
work as Brockman and Peter had hoped they might.

Students, too, entered actively into the effort. In 1915, Tientsin students distributed 100,000 public health circulars throughout the city, and six hundred students "with brass bands and banners" marched in a parade and gave street corner lectures on the dangers of tuberculosis. In Hangchow, night school students distributed pamphlets on flies.[58] In Changsha and Peking, students conducted lantern slide campaigns—lecturing in Changsha alone to over ten thousand people.[59] A staff trained by Peter subsequently trained five hundred students in Tientsin and seventy-five students in Changsha to be a special "health faculty," which could itself conduct campaigns.[60]

The education was not one-sided, for as Peter and his assistants gained more experience, they recognized the sources of Chinese community spirit. Concern for others was not lacking, but appeals that would work in America would not work in China. For instance, when Peter demonstrated with his flashing lights and falling skulls that huge numbers of Chinese were dying each year because of overcrowding, poor sanitation, and contagion, the retort invariably came that China had too many people anyway, and that a good crop of deaths every year was all that kept people from being pushed into the sea. On the other hand, audiences responded enthusiastically to the suggestion that public health contributed to national power. So compelling was this argument, especially after the Twenty-One Demands of Japan were made known in May 1915, that Peter discarded all other themes and concentrated on "The Relationship of National Health to National Strength." [61] This appeal elicited a powerful affirmative response.

Peter's account of the enthusiasm with which thousands of Chinese greeted his campaigns leads to the same conclusion as do the accounts of student social service work during these years, namely, that the Chinese—at least a great many of the upper and middle class Chinese—were already eager to participate in moderate social reform. There was some basis for a sense of community responsibility. It cannot be claimed that any single organization had produced this new, if slight, sense of community responsibility, which was rather owing to the upheavals of the century. But the Y.M.C.A. had, at the very least, discovered one way to awaken and discipline the new spirit. The Association not only recognized the compelling themes of Chinese concern but also developed new tools for public organization and persuasion. Popular propaganda campaigns were potentially powerful weapons for stirring the community to humanitarian service. They were usable in other causes as well. On June 17, 1915, for instance, three thousand Peking students subsidized by a Y.M.C.A. benefactor named Frank Yung Tao paraded through the city to a downtown park where they held a five-hour rally, lecturing before a large crowd on "moral and social reform," by which they meant an end to political corruption.[62] It required no special insight to see that mass communication could be put to the service of causes other than health. This possibility the Association itself realized and now turned its attention to other such causes.

Aware that the technique of mass persuasion could be applied to many ends, the Association in 1915 started a Conservation Division, headed by D. Y. Lin (Lin Dau-yang), which was intended to stir interest in reforestation.[63] The area most profoundly expressing both Western liberal faith and the mainstream of Chinese tradition, however, was education itself. Literacy, the Association believed, was the key to opening many doors. A literate man was more powerful and productive than an illiterate one. If popular lectures could persuade the Chinese community to work not only for public health but also for education, the Association would have played a significant part in benefiting China. Acting upon earlier plans, the Lecture Bureau formally initiated an Education Division in 1915 and named David Yui as its director. Yui, holder of a Masters' Degree in Education from Harvard, planned a campaign to enlist public support for more schools.

By 1915 modern education had made some progress in China. The reality by no means fit the elaborate plans drawn up by the central government, which in 1914 had set out on paper a system of schools ranging from elementary to university level, and in 1916 began to emphasize elementary education. Yet the school system was expanding. There were approximately 120,000 government schools of various kinds, serving about 4,000,000 students out of an estimated 89,000,000 children of school age. Among the schools were over 3,000 government and technical institutions, with a handful of special schools for the handicapped. Mission schools included almost 500,000 students.[64] Most of these enterprises, however, were aimed at the middle class, which could afford to send children to school instead of putting them to work. Young merchant apprentices, the urban proletariat, and virtually the entire rural population remained illiterate.

Here and there, scattered efforts were being made to reduce illiteracy. Educators were experimenting with lists of basic characters and with various phonetic systems for teaching reading. Social service work by students connected with the Y.M.C.A. had resulted in a few schools for youngsters. In 1914 the Tientsin Association opened another such school. In Hangchow, Eugene Barnett established several summer schools for illiterates, taught by student volunteers. Such work was possible not only because of student cooperation but because of community assistance as well. One of the Hangchow school sites was the primary school building of the Silk Guild, Barnett being a good friend of the guild president, as well as of the police commissioner and several Buddhist priests who were Association members. The police commissioner even decided to open a school for illiterates himself, using officers as teachers.[65] In Chengtu a school was established under Association auspices, where illiterates were taught to read, write the most common characters, and do simple arithmetic.[66]

A variant of such work was also underway in Kirin, Manchuria. There, Y.M.C.A. Secretary Orrin Magill had been particularly attracted by the "bright, intelligent faces" of young merchant apprentices in the city's shops and stores. Upon investigation, he found that they were virtually prisoners in the shops, not allowed to sit during the day or to leave the shop at any time, receiving no wages and almost no education beyond use of the abacus. Magill decided to experiment with night school education for the youngsters. After a total lack of success with their employers, whom he characterized as "grasping and suspicious," he enlisted the aid of a young merchant with influence in the commercial guild and, through this personal friendship, got a group of boys released every weekday evening for lessons.[67]

The existence of a few part-time schools produced barely a splash in the ocean of illiteracy. Yet such developments indicated that given the proper push, people in the community would cooperate in widening educational opportunities and, further, that many people deprived of such opportunities were interested in learning to read. The Y.M.C.A. determined to use the popular lecture technique in a huge campaign to mobilize the public. The Visual Aids Department of the Lecture Bureau prepared models of men equipped with buttons that made their eyes shine and their heads expand with the power of education, and levers that made a man grow feet taller as he learned to read. On a large board were listed the names of China, Japan, Germany, and the United States, with a button that caused a ribbon to pop out showing the amount of illiteracy in each country. The ribbons for Japan, the United States, and Germany were barely visible, but when the demonstrator pressed the button for China, the ribbon zoomed thirty feet over the heads of the audience.[68] These aids were put at Yui's disposal.

For Yui, the lecture series presented only one of many challenges. C. T. Wang had returned to government service early in 1916, whereupon Yui was named acting general secretary of the Chinese Association. He now became concerned with finances, missionary relations, administration of the bustling city Associations, the nagging problem of unsupervised student Associations, and dozens of other executive problems. Even the lecture bureau itself presented a problem, for with World War I in full swing, American support was being diverted from lectures in China to aid to Europe. Despite these added burdens, however, Yui plunged vigorously into a series of lectures on China's need for education.

The government and educators throughout the major cities were not only cordial but anxious to hear Yui. On his inaugural tour he visited Peking at the request of the Ministry of Education, which was trying to set up a lecture series. The ministry, hoping to encourage local leaders to establish schools, requested duplicates of Yui's visual aids. In Peking and Tientsin Yui lectured before the Ministries of Agriculture and Commerce, many educators, and students at several schools. Old Yen Hsiu, sponsor of the Nankai Middle School, went to hear him in Tientsin. In Tungchow the local magistrate asked Yui to give a special lecture for village heads within twenty li of the town. In Tsinan, the governor asked him to lecture before the electors assembled to represent Shantung in the prospective national assembly. Similar receptions were held in Nanking, Soochow, Foochow, Changchow, Amoy, and Shanghai. By the middle of 1917 the national Ministry of Education and the governors of several provinces had asked Yui to organize an educational lecturers' institute in Shanghai, so that other men might duplicate his work throughout China. Forty men were sent to the institute: twenty-two from Kiangsu, five from Shantung, four from Chekiang, two from Chihli, two from the Ministry of Education in Peking, and five from the district educational associations already existing in Kiangsu, plus thirteen special students who intended to work privately. Yui trained these men for a month in the theory of education and the techniques of popular lectures. By year's end, Yui himself had lectured in thirty cities, and some of the men he had trained were spread through Kiangsu and Shantung, duplicating his work. Yui claimed a total attendance of almost a quarter of a million people at these lectures.[69]

The texts of the lectures no longer exist. It is known of them only that Yui hammered at the theme that a strong country must have a literate people.[70] He was a compelling speaker, with one major advantage over C. H. Robertson and W. W. Peter: he was Chinese. His success with lectures, widely acknowledged in later years as Robertson's and Peter's success was not, showed that China held to her traditional belief in the need for education. A great many people obviously wanted to come to grips with the problem.

But goodwill, interest, and public sympathy did not suffice to solve the problem. The illiterate population was enormous. China could not transport millions of children overnight to neat schoolhouses that did not exist. There was a paucity of trained teachers. Furthermore, education took time. Vaccinating a child required only a moment, whereas teaching him to read took years. Both money and time were necessary before China could have a professional, national school system that would reach the bulk of her population. All that Yui could hope for was to persuade the Chinese leaders and middle class to support the long effort necessary to produce such a system. However, there were indications that ingenuity might provide a voluntary transitional education program which would fill the gap while a professional system was being designed, for from James Yen, working with Chinese laborers in France, came evidence that illiterates could and would learn to read, and in China itself, signs appeared that nonprofessional teachers could play a helpful role by penetrating the world of illiterates far more deeply than anyone had realized. A series of minor new successes in popular education fused with the techniques of persuasion and social organization already developed by the Y.M.C.A. to produce the mass education movement.

Sent to France by the Y.M.C.A., James Yen and other Chinese volunteers carried on a remarkable work of education for illiterate Chinese laborers during World War I.[71] By the end of 1918, more than 140,000 Chinese were at work on French soil unloading ships, constructing camps, digging roads, and reburying the dead. Forty thousand of these men were in French employ, free to come and go as they pleased except for certain travel restrictions. But those Chinese under the British system were isolated in special camps without recreational facilities. Y.M.C.A. investigators reported that the men spent their spare time gambling, discussing the lack of harmony between the earth and air, worrying about possibly permanent enslavement in the trenches, and wondering what was happening in the world outside the camp. Since 80 percent of the men were illiterate, most had no means of communication with their families and no way of receiving news. The Y.M.C.A. obtained permission to offer services to the men, and by the end of 1918 there were eighty Y.M.C.A. huts in camps throughout France where the men could drink tea and smoke, play chess, put on amateur theatricals, have letters written, and engage in sports. Missionaries and Western Y.M.C.A. workers from China staffed a few of the camps, but most of the work was carried on by Chinese students recruited from American universities. Yen was one such volunteer; others were Daniel Fu, later a Y.M.C.A. worker in China, and T. F. Tsiang, afterwards an ambassador to the United States. Fu and Yen established elementary schools in their huts, to teach illiterates several hundred common characters, and Yen also started in Bologne a mimeographed news sheet in the vernacular entitled "Chu-fa Hua-kung Chou-pao" or "The Laborers' Weekly." [72] The paper was simple and practical, containing news and admonitions not to drink or gamble.

Yen had never before experienced contact with Chinese coolies or laborers as human beings.[73] As he now worked with them, he began to like them, and the more he got to know them, the more his liking grew. It was in France, friends later recalled, that Yen began to argue that the real Chinese citizen was not a scholar, an official, or a member of the gentry, but a laborer or a farmer.[74] As Yen observed the response to the elementary education courses, he came to feel that the illiterate yearned to break the bonds of ignorance that restricted him to a narrow world. "This intimate contact with the so-called 'Lower Classes,'" he wrote a few years later about the peasants, ". . . revealed to them [i.e., to the Chinese Y.M.C.A. workers in France] . . . the undreamed-of possibilities in these men and . . . the gigantic problem of the illiterate millions confronting their home land. Right there and then they decided to give their lives to the task of educating and uplifting the masses." [75]

The secretaries G. H. Cole, W. W. Peter, and Roscoe Hersey were also in France at this time, on loan from the Chinese Y.M.C.A. Cole, and perhaps the others, talked over with Yen the possibilities of using visual aid techniques such as slides to teach characters to the men.[76] Although Cole acquired twenty slide projectors and many slides on Western culture for the use of the secretaries, this technique was not adopted in the laborers' literacy program.[77] Instead, the Chinese secretaries used more conventional methods, although they added a phonetic system to the traditional task of memorizing characters. Yen was made aware, however, that professional visual techniques were available to help in the anticipated work of mass education. As he saw the literacy of the laborers creep up to 38 percent, his enthusiasm mounted.

In Shanghai another Y.M.C.A. secretary was also coming to the conclusion that nonprofessional teachers could instruct illiterates. One of the boys' secretaries, J. C. Clark, was touched by the life of boys in the business world. He, like Orrin Magill in Kirin a few years before, had found that many apprentices worked fifteen to eighteen hours a day and rarely learned to read or write. During 1919 the Shanghai Y.M.C.A. opened huts for these youngsters. Clark, realizing that students could help him in his work, began in June to train several of them to teach classes, run games, give health talks, and lead singing. It was a variation of the "Big Brother" movement in the United States. Clark did not, however, stop with students. He started a "Social Improvement Club" that depended on the boys themselves. They in turn became teachers for people in their immediate neighborhood, first teaching other neighborhood youngsters to play, then telling them stories about health or patriotism. As an added feature of the club, the boys who were receiving actual instruction in the Association clubs or classes started a "Home Student Movement" to teach people who could not get to the Association building, such as other children in the family or servants. Clark had high hopes for what these young teachers might accomplish. Within the year he was making plans to start a boy teacher movement that would encompass three hundred blocks in Shanghai and eventually the entire city, teaching lessons on fly-killing, citizenship, vaccination, and education through phonetics.[78]

By 1920, therefore, several choices of teaching methods and of utilizing stopgap teachers had suggested themselves. With proper organization, many other kinds of people in the community could evidently be counted upon to give their support. That an entire community could be organized in its own interest was unquestionable, for Dr. Peter and his staff had just successfully conducted a week-long campaign in Foochow to prevent an anticipated cholera outbreak. Through parades, student lecturers, slide presentations, idols named "Mr. Cholera," canvassing of stores, boats, and restaurants, and through wholesale official cooperation, they had succeeded in getting people to screen their food, boil water, and take other necessary precautions.[79] Furthermore, the time seemed ripe for the Y.M.C.A. to sponsor a new educational experiment, for its popularity had never been so high. Its work with laborers in France had elicited considerable enthusiasm and financial support from China. Statistics reinforced the optmism, for by the beginning of 1920 the Association included 46,000 members, and Chinese fees and donations for the year amounted to half a million dollars.

David Yui therefore agreed to put the Association's energy

and resources behind a mass education experiment. At the end of 1920 Yen returned from a year at Princeton Graduate School and began to work out a basic education plan involving one thousand common characters. For this enterprise he had the cooperation and guidance of Professors H. C. Chen and T'ao Hsing-chih, both of the Nanking National Teachers College (Nan-ching Kao-teng Shih-fan Hsüeh-hsiao). As a result, Yen produced a series of elementary primers utilizing the most common vernacular characters, called "People's Thousand Character Lesson" (P'ing-min Ch'ien-tzu k'o).[80] As this work proceeded, Yen discussed with Yui and other Association secretaries where and how the work should begin.

Yen himself had originally hoped to carry on the experiment in his own province of Szechwan, but Yui persuaded him that the work demanded an area more attuned to modern needs, as well as one where the Association itself had a more pervasive network of influence.[81] The obvious place to begin at first seemed to be Shanghai, where the Association was strong, and a literacy program promised to reach the laboring and industrial classes. In Shanghai and a few other cities, the Association had already put up huts to serve industrial workers, many of whom were returned laborers from France. Aware of the rising tide of open hostility between capital and labor, the Y.M.C.A. was moving belatedly into industrial work, hoping to retain its traditional neutrality and to provide a service program of health, education, and recreation. Secretaries, puzzled and disturbed at the antagonism between capital and newly organized labor, were falling back on their faith in bringing to the laboring class "enlightenment and service which would help make them better citizens." [82] A mass education experiment in Shanghai might serve that purpose.

Practicalities, however, soon changed both the locale and the emphasis. Shanghai secretaries J. C. Clark and Lawrence

Hall, both experienced in community organization and work with illiterates, persuaded Yen that his first experiment should be among apprentice boys rather than adults, since youngsters learned more quickly. Furthermore, because community cooperation was so important, they felt that Yen should begin in a smaller city that could be totally mobilized by the Association's varied techniques. Harold Rounds of the Changsha Association promised to help, and in the spring of 1921 Hall and Yen went to Changsha to mobilize the community for the first mass education experiment in China.[83]

There is no more dramatic way to record the Changsha experiment than to quote Yen himself at length on this first campaign:

The purpose of the campaign was to start a forward movement toward making Changsha 100% literate by arousing popular enthusiasm for the idea [of mass education]. The goal originally chosen for the first term was "One thousand illiterates to learn to read and write one thousand characters in four months" by spending one to one and a half hours each weekday.

A general committee of seventy leading members of the city, representing business men, college presidents, editors, officials, guild leaders, pastors, teachers, and students, was organized. Out of this general committee five subcommittees, on finance, recruiting teachers, recruiting pupils, securing classrooms and publicity respectively, were appointed to set up the campaign.

Publicity:

For purposes of publicity the following means were used:
1. Fifteen hundred posters, picturing China's problem of illiteracy and need of education.

160

2. Five hundred official proclamations issued by the Governor, urging all citizens who have illiterate children or apprentices to avail themselves of the opportunity to learn.

3. Twenty-six thousand dodgers "exhorting education," giving necessary information concerning the "Foundation Character Schools."

4. Daily newspaper material to the newspapers.

5. Two large meetings of shop-masters, chiefly from the manual trades.

6. Mass meeting for the city with the governor presiding.

7. A general parade by college and middle school students, who carried large banners and lanterns with such suggestive and appealing sentences as these: "An illiterate man is a blind man," "Is your son blind?" "An illiterate nation is a weak nation," "China's salvation? Popular education," "Can you endure to see three fourths of China go blind?"

Recruiting:

For recruiting purposes the city was divided into seventy-five districts. Teams of students were organized, trained and sent with registration card and other necessary literature to visit the shops and homes, one by one, district by district. The work was surprisingly successful. Recruiting had to be called off after two-thirds of the districts were canvassed, for in three afternoons the teams recruited 1400 men and boys.

Eighty teachers were recruited from the teaching staff of government, mission, and private schools. These teachers kept on with their regular school work during the day and taught one and a half hours each evening. They received no salary, but $4.00 per month was allowed each for ricksha fare. Because of the special requirements several training classes in methods of teaching, conducting games and singing were held for these volunteer teachers. In their work they devoted one hour each evening to the lesson and the rest of the time was divided between moral addresses, singing and playing.

School Buildings:

Over sixty buildings were secured in all sections of the city. Primary schools, churches, guild halls, temples, club houses, private residences, police stations, and the Y.M.C.A. were all utilized. The teachers themselves elected the president and four supervisors. These in turn were assisted by secretaries to provide the necessary supervision. One of the devices used for encouraging study and attendance was the wearing of badges which were graded according to the colors of the Chinese flag. Successful students of the monthly examination were awarded one of the badges according to the number of characters they learned; miniature monthly commencement exercises were held to which students, shop masters, families and friends were invited.

Commencement:

The school term lasted from March to July 1922. Of the 1400 enrolled, 1200 boys and men attended the classes to the very last day of the term and took the final examination. Nine hundred sixty-seven passed successfully and were given certificates by the Governor of the Province on the 20th of July when the graduating exercises were elaborately celebrated.

A study of the twelve hundred boys and men shows that their ages ranged from six to forty-two years. The significant fact, however, is that 81.1% of the entire student body were between the ages of ten and twenty . . . It is indeed fortunate that this most needy and most "mouldable" group should be at the same time the most accessible. Ten years hence they will be the very members who will play their part in shaping the destiny of the nation. So, while it is not possible to cover the three hundred million illiterates all at once, it is good strategy to concentrate the attack, principally though not entirely, upon these youths.[84]

In September of the same year, Changsha enrolled over fifteen hundred new illiterates in another mass education session. Chefoo and Hangchow followed suit with equally impressive results, and Yen began to extend both the scope and variety of the classes. Gentry and business people as well as professional teachers volunteered to teach. Girls were allowed into the classes. Yen used slide projectors to teach classes of from two to five hundred students at once.[85] Available to him now were a great variety of teaching methods, ranging from the "little teacher" system in Shanghai, to mobile schools that could help illiterates whose occupations forced them to move from place to place. Already he dreamed of taking the program into the countryside. The program, he wrote, "will and must emanate from the middle class." [86]

For the first time in the modern era, Chinese society seemed to be mobilizing its resources to make a fundamental change. Within a year one province after another began to adopt the mass education movement. Over two million copies of the "People's Thousand Character Lesson" primers were sold; self-supporting mass education movements arose in city after city; and in 1923 China's most distinguished educators, among them Hu Shih, Chang Po-ling, and T'ao Hsing-chih, met with Yen at Tsing Hua University to form the National Mass Education Association (Chung-kuo P'ing-min Chiao-yü Ts'u-chin Tsung-hui).[87] Optimism rose high.

As the new movement spread, C. H. Robertson took note of it. "In twenty years in China nothing has impressed me more than the mass educational movement now developing," he wrote. "A great light begins to shine in Asia. I believe it will reach in beneficent and healing rays around a dark and needy world."[88] As missionaries had long hoped, a contagion for reform seemed at last to have infected China. It was not Christianity that was spreading, but the liberation of men's minds from illiteracy. This accomplishment, the Y.M.C.A. still believed, would achieve China's salvation, and the Association was justly proud of the part it had played.

Even as plans were being made for the mass education movement to spread into the countryside, new forces were at work. Leaders in the era following the revolution had admired the accomplishments of the West, tolerated a mild aura of Christianity, and respected the Y.M.C.A. for its accomplishments rather than castigating it for its omissions. But the times were changing, and new contenders for the hearts of Chinese youth were beginning to appear. A second tide of revolution was rising in China, which this time threatened to engulf the Chinese Y.M.C.A.

6

STUDENTS AND REVOLUTION

As the mass campaigns showed, thousands of adult middle-class Chinese were willing to support the goals of the Y.M.C.A. and to give it financial backing. While courting this stable constituency before 1920, however, the Y.M.C.A. had been neglecting the students who once were its main reason for existence. In the early 1920's this neglect led to a serious problem. Swept up by nationalism and by revolutionary political movements, aroused by militant student unions and the Communist party, buffeted by new ideas, students began to see the Y.M.C.A. as a tool of the bourgeoisie, irrelevant and even inimical to Chinese needs. Virulent propaganda by radical political organizations purported to identify the Association as a weapon of imperialism. Anti-Christian groups found sinister meaning in the organization's religious affiliations. The amicable climate within which the Association had flourished was changing rapidly.

Faced with this new revolutionary atmosphere, the Association floundered. Its attempts to understand the temper of the 1920's were belated and only partly successful. The question was revived as to whom the organization should serve. It faced the difficult task of being both patriotic and international, Christian and revolutionary, spokesman for the community and also for the young. It must respond to the times and yet preserve its familiar identity. The Association was neither unimaginative nor inflexible, but fast as it moved to meet these needs, China was moving even faster. As the decade wore on and other groups joined the attack, the question became not one of success, but of survival. By the end of 1926, the Y.M.C.A. realized with dismay that the price of survival might be prohibitive.

In 1919 these problems were still obscured by evidences of success, for membership rolls and receipts continued to rise. Although a few secretaries were already warning about the neglect of student work, they were largely ignored, for the Association's unofficial cooperation with the May Fourth movement at first seemed to keep it in the mainstream of student activity. When the boycott movement started, several secretaries foresaw that the Association would forfeit student confidence if it followed the hands-off policy adopted by formal church groups. But active participation was dangerous, since support for the boycotts might mean retaliation by the Peking government. In addition, the international Y.M.C.A. maintained a substantial program in Japan that might be jeopardized by anti-Japanese statements. The Association therefore attempted to pass itself off as a peacemaker, preserving a facade of neutrality. In Shanghai, staff leaders organized a Christian patriotic movement that enlisted not only Christian groups but also the provincial education association and the Shanghai Student Union. This group worked to keep relations cordial between Westerners and the student union.[1] Moreover, the Association disclaimed any formal relationship with student activists. When students at the Shanghai Y.M.C.A. Middle School formed a branch of the student union and produced a "Y.M.C.A." boycott stamp with the words, "This store doesn't import Japanese goods," the Y.M.C.A. declared that it did not sponsor either the union or the boycott.[2]

Such disclaimers, however, masked not only sympathy but also support. The Shanghai Middle School Student Union held its meetings at the Association building.[3] In Peking, the young secretary Hsu Pao-ch'ien, once president of the Peking Social Service Club (Pei-ching She-hui Shih-chin hui), was asked to participate in discussions held by boycott leaders. Many Peking officials were even said to believe that the Y.M.C.A. was generally responsible for arranging the original student march —"an honor," wrote Peking Secretary Dwight Edwards, "which only a sense of truth and modesty prevents us from appreciating." Reporting on boycott movements elsewhere, Edwards observed, "Y.M.C.A. secretaries were frequently in close touch with the student soviets. Some Association buildings were used as centers by the students." [4] Thus, the Association still felt in close harmony with students.

The early wave of Y.M.C.A. popularity with the students soon subsided, however, as the Association continued to maintain official neutrality and to insist on moderation. Students wanted clear-cut positions and concrete assistance. "Students look to us for leadership," a report declared. "It's hard to explain to them why we can't join them in political agitation." [5] To the more intransigent students, any attempt to hold a middle ground position was beginning to resemble cowardice, if not treachery. Thus, by 1920 an undercurrent of student discontent was developing.

As the May Fourth movement continued, overt difficulties appeared. The original student focus on nationalism broadened to include a variety of challenges to the established political, social, and intellectual values of the middle class. With some of these challenges directed at values deeply imbedded in Y.M.C.A. tradition, the Association's response was not entirely favorable. David Yui was completely in favor of working with the movement but agreed that some aspects posed a threat to Chinese civilization. "We should lend our support," he wrote, "but should also try to Christianize the movement." [6] Another secretary, H. A. Wilbur, declared that the spirit of the youths around him denoted a strongly patriotic, mostly unselfish, enquiring generation, but he also found that some of their activities were "ill-considered." [7] The Asso-

martin Wilbur's father?

ciation could give only partial approval to the movement's objectives and techniques.

One aspect of the May Fourth movement was a growing concern among the young for the plight of labor. Many students had first been seriously aroused to the troubles of the urban poor by the Y.M.C.A. itself, through its seminars, lectures, and social service work. Even nonparticipants had been led to believe that Christian organizations were passionately concerned with the poor. Now the Association's more thoughtful and serious student members wanted to know what part the organization planned to take in rectifying social injustice. What good was a Christian organization that seemed unwilling to face the problems of industrial exploitation? What did Christianity mean if Christian leaders were silent on social, industrial, and intellectual questions? John Childs wrote from Peking that students would not heed a religion that stayed out of the social arena.[8] He made pointed reference to the Association's hesitation and confusion over labor problems, a timidity that was damaging its reputation as an innovator in the community.

The parent Association in the United States had long ignored labor problems, partly because the American Y.M.C.A. counted on the backing of bankers, partly because staff members were not trained to think about the social implications of economic change. The historian Owen Pence has written: "The Association served the rank and file of a growing middle class constituency that accepted both the ideologies and the services born of the industrial transformation of the common life. It apparently did so uncritically."[9]

This traditional avoidance of economic problems had carried over to China for many of the same reasons. Both Western and Chinese secretaries were members of the middle class and generally accepted the need to work within the prevailing system. Gradualists, they did not believe that major changes could be accomplished quickly. Typical of their attitude was a statement made by David Yui in 1920 to about eight hundred students leaving for the United States. After their return, he told them, they should not attempt ambitious projects of national importance, but should do their work quietly.[10] Recognition would come in time.

This commitment to gradualism and the Association's timidity toward the unfamiliar, combined with its limited resources, had kept the Chinese Association out of industrial work, despite expressions of concern that went as far back as 1912. By 1920, however, the need for some kind of industrial effort was being underscored by the return of Chinese laborers from France. Although most of these laborers were reabsorbed into the life of their villages, many also went to the cities looking for jobs. Accustomed to Association services in France, they turned to the Y.M.CA. for help. With the appearance of an industrial proletariat and of labor unions presaging an era of militant labor organization, many merchants and industrialists were unwilling to hire the repatriates, especially since laborers in France had been involved in several strikes. It was reported that merchants and urban leaders considered the men "too wise and in danger of causing trouble." [11] There seemed little opportunity for the Association to help these workers find jobs, yet it felt the need to play a role in the changing industrial society.

The first response of the Association reflected its tradition of self-help. Experiments with the growing labor class in Wuhan centered around plans for clubs that would provide education, recreation, and lessons on thrift and citizenship. Secretaries in that city started a center for workingmen, imitating the experience in France by offering an athletic, religious, and educational program. In Shanghai secretaries began an extension program of recreation and education in seven factories, besides operating free schools for the children of factory workers, rickshaw coolies, and laundrymen.[12] Commendable as these efforts were, they compared to using a water pistol against a forest fire. Secretary William Lockwood of Shanghai confessed that none of the staff knew how to design a program to serve the needs of labor. He knew that workers were desperately poor and that militant unions were arising, but all the Association could suggest were the familiar methods of paternalism and self-improvement. The dimensions of Lockwood's naiveté emerge from his statement: "Had we been able to go into Russia with our city and student program, had we been able to follow this ten years ago with an industrial and rural program, the history of the world would be different." [13]

The Association faced a dilemma. Aside from its inexperience with labor movements, it relied financially on the very class whom laborers were challenging. The industrialists of the country, while willing in some cases to sponsor a recreation program or free night classes, were not willing to conspire at what they considered their own extinction. At an Association-sponsored industrial conference in 1920, secretaries heard a number of sharp comments. "I promote a man, raise him to a dollar a day, then he says I am a different man. I see then that I have practically trained other people's weapons to kill me." So said the general manager of the Yangtze Engineering Works. The manager of the Hanyang Iron Works pointed out that if he reduced the workday to six hours, laborers would simply spend their new leisure in dissipation and would be

170

just as tired as if they had worked twelve. The task of the Y.M.C.A., he suggested, was to let laborers know why they could not take the place of management.[14]

In the face of such responses, the Association moved cautiously. At its 1920 national convention it failed to take a firm stand on labor problems, for which it was berated by Frank Rawlinson, influential editor of *The Chinese Recorder*.[15] In February 1921, David Yui wrote only that the Association must try to create a sense of responsibility and to bring enlightenment and services to the workers so as to make them better citizens.[16] The Association's conservatism was further emphasized in a memorandum from William Lockwood. According to him, its industrial work should be a cooperative employer-employee effort, using men and boys within mills or factories to carry on voluntary service. Secretaries should be assigned to such work who knew the relationship of economics and sociology to capital. But, he continued, "We believe that the Association should not take part in discussion of questions that are issues between the employers and employees, but should in its program in the mill or factory confine itself to questions that fall within the recognized province of the Association." This policy left unanswered, he admitted, the question of exactly what part the Association should play in helping to create better conditions for the laborer. "It is very difficult and will be increasingly so not to identify ourselves with either one side or the other . . . and to keep the building from being the meeting place of . . . the labor agitator or . . . of the capitalist." [17]

In Shanghai in May 1922, the National Christian Conference recommended an eight-hour day and a weekly day of rest for workers, prohibition of child labor under the age of twelve, "proper" working conditions, and a "living wage." Association leaders who had attended the conference announced that they "preferred to engage in constructive work rather than agitate for the immediate realization of such unrealistic visions." [18] Whatever the practicality of such a position, it was not calculated to gain the confidence either of workers or of impatient students who wanted immediate changes. Many concluded that the Association "must sing the song of him whose bread he eats." [19]

Prodded by a few staff members to approach labor problems systematically, the Association finally secured the services of a Scottish-trained engineer, M. T. (Thomas) Tchou. Tchou embarked on an ambitious industrial and labor survey of Chinese cities. His conclusions were gloomy, offering no simple solutions. The serious labor problem would improve, he stated, only when China's resources were better developed. Meanwhile, his immediate suggestion remained basically that of uplift: thrift lessons, the establishment of savings societies, and an end to drinking, smoking, and gambling.[20] More sophisticated secretaries sniffed at such nostrums. John Childs called for vigorous mobilization of public opinion to secure labor legislation, and John Stewart Burgess declared, "The salvation of men depends not only on the saving of individuals but on the saving and transformation of the whole social fabric." [21] These cries, however, went largely disregarded. At its 1923 national convention the Y.M.C.A. did hold labor panels and passed resolutions to "Christianize industry," but this was a slogan, not a program.

In a piecemeal fashion a few city Associations began to involve themselves in practical labor questions. In Kiangsu, local secretaries began to work for child labor laws, while in several cities unions were encouraged to meet in Association buildings. In Hankow, Secretary W. P. Mills served as arbitrator in a major rickshaw strike. Other secretaries tried to persuade Christian manufacturers to give workers Sundays off.[22] As a national organization, however, the Association did not know how to face the problem of labor unrest and industrial exploitation, and in many cities it ignored the problem altogether. Its influence with workers was therefore often minimal. Students increasingly accused the Y.M.C.A. of being an "upper class club." [23] The militant activism of the Communist party offered an alternative not only to laborers but also to students interested in swift and radical solutions. Shortly after the party was founded in 1921, it began to enlist students in Shanghai to organize workers, teach night schools, and guide recreation. To these techniques, similar in many respects to those of the Y.M.C.A., the party added the lure of a revolutionary ideology. More students were now interested in Karl Marx, an educator told Eugene Barnett, than in Jesus Christ.[24]

This observation pinpointed another problem beginning to haunt the Association, the growing and clamorous criticism of Christianity and Christian-related organizations. Such criticism, long a latent theme in China, was gaining strength as students attacked Christianity on both intellectual and political grounds. One hallmark of the May Fourth movement was the development of what Chow Tse-tsung has termed "the agnostic, rational, and iconoclastic tide" in which first Confucianism and then Christianity were condemned as superstitious and useless.[25] These criticisms eventually reached the Y.M.C.A. In 1920 a Chinese pastor reported to an Association conference in Nanking that students had accused religion of interfering with free thought.[26] Others reported that conventional religious teaching about personal salvation was greeted with doubt and derision, and that discussions centering around the promise of a New Kingdom to be set up in Jerusalem did not seem rational to students.[27] The spirit of agnosticism did not bode well for the Association's religious program.

Furthermore, students were being warned to avoid all connection with Christian-related institutions. The Association had first encountered this problem in France, where a number of secretaries who had arrived to work with Chinese labor gangs attempted also to organize a program for Chinese students. Many of these students had been brought to France by the avowedly atheistic and anarchistic Société Franco-Chinoise d'Education. Although most of the students were antireligious, many were friendly toward the Y.M.C.A. and eager to avail themselves of its services. Student leaders, however, had bluntly forbidden them to join the Y.M.C.A. because of its Christian affiliation. The hostility was intense. "I believe that if something could be done here," wrote one secretary, "it would be done only with the help of God." [28]

This organized hostility to Christianity was also growing inside China. Not only was Christianity attacked on intellectual grounds, but with the rise of the Communist party and of the increasingly radical student unions, propaganda appeared linking Christianity with imperialism and capitalism. In 1920 the Young China Association (Shao-nien Chung-kuo Hsüeh-hui) had attempted unsuccessfully to launch an organized antireligious movement. In 1922 a larger movement was started by a coalition of several groups, including not only the Young China Association but also anarchists, communists, and the left wing of the Kuomintang.[29] This time the Y.M.C.A. was directly attacked. In April 1922, the World Student Christian Federation was scheduled to hold a world convention in Peking, an event with which the Y.M.C.A. was intimately concerned. In March a "Declaration of the Non-Christian Stu-

174

dents Federation," couched in language derived from the Communist catechism, appeared in the newspapers. It read in part: "The capitalists of all nations . . . are taking steps, one following the other, to rush into China to carry out their plans of economic exploitation. And the present-day Christianity and the Christian Church are the vanguard of the exploitation . . . Those nations who have established the Y.M.C.A. in China have as their object nothing more than to rear up good and efficient bloodhounds of the capitalists . . . How can we not rise and oppose them when we see with our own eyes these bloodhounds of the capitalists holding a conference to discuss how to decide our fate?" [30]

Dwight Edwards noted that these federations "flooded the country" with telegrams calling on students to arise and prevent China from being led astray by Christianity.[31] The attack failed to halt the conference, but it added to the growing student reluctance to associate with Christianity or its related institutions. A postconference religious campaign attempted by student Christian leaders in twenty-seven cities was a failure. Eugene Barnett saw the anti-Christian campaign as harbinger of a future in which Christianity, imperialism, and economic exploitation would be persistently linked.[32]

The temper of the Y.M.C.A. before 1922 had been ebullient. After the Peking attack, doubt and deep pessimism emerged, nourished both by the continuing chaos in China and by a belated admission that other ideas and organizations were competing vigorously for student attention. Realizing that its own values were no longer wholeheartedly accepted even by its own constituency, the Y.M.C.A. at last looked closely at its relationship to students. In the process, staff leaders were forced to re-examine the overall direction and policies of the Association. Success, they found, exacted its own penalties. In the attempt to develop a widespread base of support, the Y.M.C.A. had also developed needs and values that might no longer be compatible with the demands of the young.

In the years since 1911 the Y.M.C.A. had achieved its objective of becoming a genuine community organization active in public health campaigns, anti-opium movements, social surveys, mass education programs, recreational activities, public lectures, and the operation of dormitories. By 1922, 54,000 members belonged to associations in 36 cities. The Y.M.C.A. employed 378 Chinese and 81 foreign secretaries in addition to its national staff.[33] This widespread and expensive operation, although supported partly by fees, depended heavily on contributions from the adult urban middle class in China and on special grants from the United States. The sensitivities of these contributors, rarely revolutionary, could not be ignored. In addition, the local Associations had to court the political favor, or at least avoid the political disfavor, of incumbent local governments, which was a risky matter. The city Associations were thus bound to established forces in the community.

Besides offering community services, the Y.M.C.A. was a genuine mass youth organization. In 1922 approximately 24,000 students were listed on its rolls as members of 200 student Associations, with an unknown number of students also using the facilities of the city Associations.[34] The very fact of membership indicated that these students approved of or at least tolerated Y.M.C.A. values. Many student members, both Christian and non-Christian, were serious and dedicated, and were deeply concerned with the problems of Chinese society.

Yet the attention paid to students was at best meager. Until 1921 there was virtually no Y.M.C.A. staff concerned specifically with student thinking or needs, for as city staff members pointed out, work with students brought in little revenue.[35] In

176

1921 the National Committee assigned two national secretaries and some thirty local secretaries to student duties. But
the official student secretaries evidently spent most of their
time worrying about organizational problems. Such educational work as they carried on specifically for students tended
to concentrate on Bible study classes, an area of growing
indifference to students. Frequently unaware of new trends in
thinking, hostile to them, or intellectually unequal to them,
student secretaries could not keep up with the ever-changing
trends of the May Fourth movement. The few dynamic local
leaders, alert to student needs, were the exceptions. In fact,
the Y.M.C.A. had lost touch with the very youth it had originally gone to China to serve.

Since the Y.M.C.A. had a traditional and emotional commitment to students, there was no real question of abandoning
student work, and there were clearly some specific improve-
ments that could be made rapidly. As temporary leader of the
Student Division, Eugene Barnett began to press energetically
for more emphasis on student work, including an expansion of
the staff and the intensive use of open forums, lectures, and
seminars on subjects interesting to the young. The Association
began to hold conferences specifically for college students. At
the 1923 national convention in Canton, a student was elected
vice-chairman of the meeting. Partly in response to student
requests, a number of panels were held on labor relations.
These unobjectionable actions constituted a step toward more
effective participation by student members.

Yet the Association was limited in its ability to meet student
demands. An organization supported largely by businessmen
could not lead a labor movement. An institution springing
from evangelical Christianity could not easily embrace religious liberalism or agnosticism. Staffs including Westerners

were unwilling to tolerate the xenophobic aspects of nationalism. An organization pledged to neutrality felt uneasy about taking any part in politics, as Sun Yat-sen had suggested at the 1923 Canton convention.[36] Secretaries asked themselves how much the Association could adapt to changing circumstances without losing its essential identity. There were no easy answers. If any continuity ran through the organization, it was a wistful hope that moderate discussion and personal integrity based on Christian values would prevail. The theme adopted for 1924 was "Character—China's Hope." But this noble statement offered little to impatient students, and more and more the Association appeared indecisive and ill at ease.

As the months wore on, Association leaders attempted further to define their role in a revolutionary China. What, a questionnaire sent to local secretaries asked, was the primary function of the Y.M.C.A. in each city and in China? Should the Association deemphasize its work with influential community members and cut down on community work in favor of student work? [37] A preliminary questionnaire for a 1925 secretaries' meeting again appealed for advice. What did Chinese youth want and what did it need? Was the Y.M.C.A. a youth movement? Should it concentrate on students? How should it cooperate with other national movements such as the student union? What should the Association do about labor? What should the program do in relation to communism, anticommunism, anticapitalism, antiimperialism? [38] As the questions poured forth, the time bomb of nationalism, antiimperialism, and anti-Christianity ticked on. On May 30, 1925, when thirteen nationalist demonstrators in Shanghai were killed by British-officered police, it exploded into a gigantic national strike in which students, merchants, and labor all participated.

This time the Association did not attempt to simulate neutrality. David Yui cabled John Mott of the United States Association to protest to the "highest authorities" about the Shanghai incident.[39] Some Associations moved to keep in touch with the boycotters and student organizations. The Shanghai staff issued a manifesto of support for the boycotts and helped to raise money and organize meetings for strikers.[40] The Y.M.C.A. publication *Chin Pu*, or *Progress*, announced that it would not carry British advertising. Western secretaries joined their Chinese colleagues in voicing anger. Some Associations responded to student demands for an exploration of other widely debated issues. In Canton the Association invited a Russian named Semenoff to present the case for communism at a public lecture—an event that enraged several of the Y.M.C.A.'s merchant backers.[41]

Nevertheless, the Y.M.C.A. found itself under attack from many quarters. The organization was widely accused of being run by the West, despite impassioned speeches by David Yui declaring that it was governed by Chinese and supported by Chinese.[42] A survey of student work in fifteen cities revealed an ebbing membership and slumping programs, and national receipts from business sources dropped sharply.[43] Even within the Y.M.C.A. some Western staff members reported hostility from Chinese colleagues.[44] Moreover, the National Student Union mounted its most virulent attack to date. In July, the seventh annual convention of the union adopted a number of resolutions concerning the Y.M.C.A. Representing an admission of the still formidable influence of the Association, these resolutions read in part:

The Y.M.C.A. and other Christian organizations and their officers are the hawks and hounds of the imperialists . . . In

the work of the Y.M.C.A. and of the churches they utilize
the name of prominent men and work together with officials
and wealthy people . . . Their aim in doing so is to poison
the spirit and deceive the minds of the Chinese youth.

During the Winter and Summer vacation Student Unions
everywhere should urge students returning to rural and
industrial districts to inform the public of the evils of Christianity. They should explain clearly . . . that the Industrial
Department of the Y.M.C.A. is an instrument used by imperialists and capitalists to cheat laborers so that they will be
contented and will regard the capitalists as their benefac-
tors who take care of them so that the laborers may be
slaves permanently. At the same time they should point out
the evil conduct of the Christians in rural districts.

Student Unions everywhere should appoint members to
enter and participate in the activities of the Y.M.C.A. and
other Christian organizations . . . Y.M.C.A.'s constantly use
athletics, popular education, etc., to do evangelistic work so
as to smother the political thoughts of the youth. They are a
detriment to the patriotic movement. Student Unions everywhere should expose them continuously . . . Student
Unions everywhere should appoint special delegates who
will try to induce Christians to leave the church and will
publish the names of Christians when they have made such
a decision.[45]

Thoroughly alarmed, David Yui called for a reevaluation of
Y.M.C.A. policies and objectives. A committee recommended
that the Association rapidly shift its main effort to concentrate
on students and industrial workers, even at the cost of sacri-
ficing established programs.[46] Yui wired the American Association for emergency funds to hire several young Chinese stu-

180

dent leaders.[47] With these decisions, the Association hoped to meet the challenge of the times.

But the times were changing so swiftly that it was not even certain there would be an opportunity to put the new program into effect. Disturbing news arrived from city after city. In Soochow, Secretary W. W. Brockman reported a massive anti-Christian movement organized by student unions and by communist representatives in the government schools. Social service club students returned religious books and dropped out of the club. Brockman was not sure that the Soochow Association could survive.[48] In Changsha, religious work came to a standstill.[49] In Swatow, a well-organized anti-Christian demonstration and parade took place on Christmas day of 1925. Student and labor union marchers scattered circulars attacking the Y.M.C.A. as a lackey of the rich and a training ground for traitors to China.[50] Furthermore, the attacks infected general community attitudes. In 1925 financial receipts fell off 15 percent from 1922. By the middle of 1926 the city Associations were facing a serious financial crisis, with membership down 13 percent from the previous year.[51]

Dismaying as these events were, the Y.M.C.A. tried to preserve a semblance of optimism. David Yui's request for funds to secure Chinese student leaders having been granted, a flow of vigorous young secretaries into the Association took place. The Association at least survived the uproar of 1925. By the end of 1926, however, survival appeared in doubt. In December 1926, Eugene Barnett and P. Y. Ma were called to Wuhan in response to an urgent telegram.[52] In Wuhan and Changsha the left wing of the Kuomintang, newly installed as the government, was carrying on a virulent anti-Christian campaign that had severely affected the Y.M.C.A. In Wuhan, the Y.M.C.A. school had closed, and the Y.M.C.A. headquarters was plastered with placards calling the Association the vanguard of imperialism. The mayor had withdrawn as head of the membership and finance campaign because of party pressure. In Changsha, Kuomintang members were forbidden to join the Y.M.C.A., and the K.M.T. had warned Y.M.C.A. members not to attend Y.M.C.A. meetings. As a result, the Association faced bankruptcy. Even more disturbing was a report that the most active anti-Christian agitators in Changsha were ex-Christian workers. Defections were particularly serious in the staff of the Bible Institute, and one Y.M.C.A. secretary resigned from the Changsha Y.M.C.A. as well as from his church to become a principal anti-Christian propagandist.

Consulting with Christian leaders in Wuhan, Barnett and Ma were told bluntly that the life of the Association was at stake. Dr. F. C. Yen, president of Hsiang-ya Medical School, told them that the communist wing of the Kuomintang could destroy any individual or institution it chose to. Francis Wei, acting president of Boone College, declared that they must find a way of identifying themselves with the revolutionary movement at once if they wished to survive. At a dinner meeting Sun Fo, head of communications of the new Kuomintang government, spelled out in more detail what this meant. He declared:

> We stand for a program of the emancipation of the poor. If this is red, then we are red. We stand for the abolition of the unequal treaties. If this is red, then we are red . . . We are against the oppressive militarists and for the people. If this is red, then we are red and as Christians must be red . . . True Christianity and the Revolution in China today are one and the same thing. Both are for the people, for the poor, for the emancipation of those who are oppressed. Only a Revolutionary Christianity can survive.

182

Soon afterward, two young Y.M.C.A. secretaries urged the Association to follow Sun's advice. "We should show that we Chinese Christians are not tools of capitalism and of cultural exploitation," remarked K. M. Yang. Paul Sung added that Christians must adopt a revolutionary spirit and begin to participate in politics. The passion for revolution clearly was not confined to students or to the Communist party; it had spread widely through Chinese society and into the Y.M.C.A. staff itself.

After his departure from Wuhan, Barnett wrote a long and thoughtful record of his observations. The main purposes of the revolution, he argued, deserved the sympathy and support of right-minded persons. Though still a minority movement, the revolution was intelligent, patriotic, and powerful, gathering the masses rapidly to its support. He sensed in the revolutionary leaders the force of an almost religious faith and passion. Those who regarded Christianity as a way of life must feel that it had a relation to the revolution.

But determining the nature of that relation was the problem. The old Y.M.C.A. policy of political neutrality could no longer suffice. At the same time, there was a powerful element in the Kuomintang that was hostile to Christianity. Remaining outside the party would stigmatize Christians as antirevolutionary, while entering the party might mean joining an anti-Christian unit. To Barnett, the central issue was: "How can we as Christians identify ourselves with the People's Revolution without compromising or repudiating our Christian loyalty?" He did not suggest an answer.

According to Barnett, the Y.M.C.A. must expect to face searching criticism—as an affiliate of Christianity, an ally of the rich, and a movement for young men but not of them. The organization was already accused of having an atmosphere "not of the dawn, but of the evening twilight." Barnett foresaw that men would be forbidden to join the Association, as had already happened in Changsha and Wuhan. Some men would choose the Kuomintang in preference to the Y.M.C.A. The Association would lose financial support, and its schools would be closed; it would be subjected to hostile propaganda, and its activities prohibited. Barnett could offer no panaceas, but felt the Association should seek to hold at least a small, hard-core membership, which believed in its values and would stand by them. This group could perhaps carry it through the storm. Barnett added: "There is all the difference in the world in the feel of the atmosphere in the present revolution and the so-called revolution of 1911. The present movement is an oceanic ground swell, not a surface disturbance, and a good deal— good and bad, one imagines—will be swept away by its oncoming tide." [53]

Despite Barnett's fears, the Chinese Y.M.C.A. was not to become an early victim of Communist enmity, for Chiang K'ai-shek was already on the march. With his victory, middle class aspirations and solutions again received official approval, and the Association took on renewed vitality. A great challenge lay ahead, for the loyalty of a whole generation was at stake. But the battle would be waged largely by Chinese, not Western, secretaries. The golden years of the West in China had come to an end.

Bibliography, Notes, Glossary and Index

SELECTED BIBLIOGRAPHY

American Board of Commissioners for Foreign Missions. "North China," vol. 4, A-B, 1880-1890. Bound documents, Houghton Library, Harvard University.

Anon. "The Present Educational Conditions in China," *Chinese Social and Political Science Review*, 5.3:298, 303 (September 1920).

Barnett, Eugene. "Autobiography." Typescript, Washington, D.C., 1962.

Beardsley, Frank Grenville. *A History of American Revivals*. New York, American Tract Society, 1912.

Biggerstaff, Knight. *The Earliest Modern Government Schools in China*. Ithaca, Cornell University Press, 1961.

————. "Shanghai Polytechnic Institution and Reading Room: An Attempt to Introduce Western Science and Technology to the Chinese," *Pacific Historical Review*, 26:127-149 (May 1956).

Birch, John Grant. *Travels in North and Central China*. London, Hurst and Blackett Ltd., 1902.

Blatt, Marilyn. "Problems of a China Missionary," *Papers on China*, 12:28-50 (1958). Harvard University, East Asian Research Center.

Blick, Judith. "The Chinese Labor Corps in World War I," *Papers on China*, 9:111-126 (1955). Harvard University, East Asian Research Center.

British Naval Staff, Intelligence Division. *Handbook of China*, vol. I, General. London, 1918.

Brockman, Fletcher. Papers, Y.M.C.A. Historical Library, New York.

————. *I Discover the Orient*. New York, Harper Bros., 1935.

Buck, Pearl. *Fighting Angel*. New York, John Day and Co., 1957. Cardinal Paperback, New York, 1964.

————. *My Several Worlds*. New York, John Day and Co., 1954.

Burgess, John Stewart. *The Guilds of Peking*. New York, Columbia University Press, 1928.

————. Papers, Y.M.C.A. Historical Library, New York.

Burton, Ernest, and Thomas C. Chamberlain. *Report of the Oriental Education Commission*. Chicago, University of Chicago, 1909.

Casserly, Capt. Gordon. *The Land of the Boxers*. London, Longmans, Green, and Co., 1903.

Chang Po-ling. Papers, Y.M.C.A. Historical Library, New York.

Chapman, J. Wilbur. *The Life and Works of Dwight L. Moody*. Philadelphia, John C. Winston and Co., 1900.

Chen Chi-yun. "Liang Ch'i-ch'ao's 'Missionary Education': A Case Study of Missionary Influence on the Reformers," *Papers on China*, 16:66-125 (1962). Harvard University, East Asian Research Center.

Cheng Yu-kwei. *Foreign Trade and Industrial Development of China*. University Press of Washington, Washington, D.C., 1956.

Chiang, Monlin. *Tides from the West*. New Haven, Yale University Press, 1947. Taipei, China Culture Publishing Foundation, 1957.

China Correspondence. Boxes 22-105, Y.M.C.A. Historical Library, New York.

China, Imperial Maritime Customs. *Decennial Reports on Trade*, Second Issue, 1892-1901, Statistical Series no. 6, vol. I. Shanghai, Inspectorate General of Customs, 1904.

China National Reports, 1895-1925. Y.M.C.A. Historical Library, New York.

The Chinese Intercollegian. Shanghai, Y.M.C.A. of China, 1897-1905.

"Chinese Laborers in France." Box of miscellaneous papers, Y.M.C.A. Historical Library, New York.

Chinese Recorder and Missionary Journal. Shanghai, American Presbyterian Press, 1877-1925.

Chinese Social and Political Science Review. Peking, Chinese Social and Political Science Association, 1916-1926.

Chow Tse-tsung. *The May Fourth Movement*. Cambridge, Mass., Harvard University Press, 1960.

Chung-hua Chi-tu-chiao ch'ing-nien hui ch'üan-kuo hsieh hui 中華基督教青年會全國協會 (Chinese Y.M.C.A. National Committee). *Chung-hua Chi-tu-chiao ch'ing-nien hui wu-shih chou-nien chi-nien ts'e* 中華基督教青年會五十周年紀念冊 (Memento of the fiftieth anniversary of the Chinese Y.M.C.A.). Shanghai, 1935.

Colquhoun, Archibald. *Overland to China*. New York, Harper and Bros., 1900.

Cohen, Paul A. *China and Christianity*. Cambridge, Mass., Harvard University Press, 1963.

Degler, Carl N. *Out of Our Past*. New York, Harper Colophon Books, 1962.

Eberhard, Wolfram. "Data on the Structure of the Chinese City in the Pre-Industrial Period," *Economic Development and Cultural Change*, 4.3:253-268 (April 1956).

Edwards, Dwight W. Papers, Y.M.C.A. Historical Library, New York.

Fairbank, John K., Edwin O. Reischauer, and Albert M. Craig. *East Asia: The Modern Transformation*. Boston, Houghton Mifflin Co., 1965.

Fisher, Daniel W. *Calvin Wilson Mateer*. Philadelphia, Westminster Press, 1911.

Foster, Mrs. Arnold. *Chinese Schoolgirls*. London, London Missionary Society, 1909.

Foster, Hon. John W. "Present Conditions in China," *National Geographic*, 17.12:651-672, 709-711 (December 1906).

Gailey, Robert R. "The Chinese Y.M.C.A.'s in 1899, The Second National Convention," *Chinese Intercollegian* (English Supplement, June 1899), p. 509.

Gregg, Alice. *China and Educational Autonomy*. Syracuse, N.Y., University of Syracuse, 1946.

Hanson, John Wesley. *The Wonderful Life and Works of Dwight L. Moody*. Atlanta, Ga., Franklin Printing and Publishing Co., n.d.

Harvard University. "Conference on the Chinese Revolution of 1911." Mimeographed proceedings, Portsmouth, N.H., 1965.

Hersey, Roscoe M. *Social Service*. 3rd ed. Shanghai, Y.M.C.A. of China, 1914.

History of the Tientsin Y.M.C.A. and Related Papers, 1897 notebook containing assorted memoranda and clippings, in D. W. Lyon Papers, Y.M.C.A. Historical Library, New York.

Hopkins, C. Howard. *History of the Y.M.C.A. in North America*. New York, Association Press, 1951.

Huang I-feng 黃逸峰. "Kuan-yü chiu Chung-kuo mai-pan chieh-chi ti yen-chiu" 关于旧中国買辦階級的研究 (Studies of old China's comprador class), *Li Shih Yen Chiu*, no. 3 (1964), pp. 89-116.

Hummel, Arthur W., ed. *Eminent Chinese of the Ch'ing Period, 1644-1912.* 2 vols. Washington, D.C., U.S. Gov. Printing Office, 1943-1944.

The Intercollegian. New York, 1890. Student Department, International Committee, and Student Volunteer Movement for Foreign Missions, published 1867. Called *The North American Student*, 1913-1918.

Kiang Kang-hu. *China and the Social Revolution*. San Francisco, Chinese Socialist Club, 1914.

Lacy, Walter N. *A Hundred Years of China Methodism*. New York, Abingdon Cokesbury Press, 1948.

Latourette, Kenneth. *World Service*. New York, Association Press, 1957.

Leong, Y. K., and L. K. Tao. *Village and Town Life in China*. London, Allen and Unwin, 1915.

Leung, S. C. "Sino-American Cooperation in Y.M.C.A. Work." Mimeographed, New York, Y.M.C.A., November 1963.

Levy, Marion J., Jr. *The Family Revolution in Modern China*. Cambridge, Mass., Harvard University Press, 1949.

Lewis, Robert. Untitled, unpaged manuscript at Y.M.C.A. Historical Library, New York, catalogued in World Service, China (X 970.4).

Li Chien-nung. *The Political History of China, 1840-1928*. Tr. Ssu-yu Teng and Jeremy Ingalls. Princeton, D. Van Nostrand, 1956.

Li Shih Yen Chiu 歷史研究 (Journal of historical studies). Peking, 1954-1964.

Lockwood, William W. Papers in Collection of W. W. Lockwood, Jr., Princeton, N.J.

Lowry, David B. "Luther D. Wishard." A.B. thesis, Princeton University, 1951.

Lyon, D. W. *Chinese Students in Japan*. Shanghai, General Committee of the Y.M.C.A. of China, Korea, and Hongkong, 1906.

———. *The First Quarter Century of the Young Men's Christian Association in China*. Shanghai, Association Press of China, 1920. Papers, Y.M.C.A. Historical Library, New York.

McCloy, C. H. *Physical Education in China*. Peking, Chinese National Association for the Advancement of Education, 1923.

Mott, John R. *The Chinese Student Migration to Tokyo*. New York, Association Press, 1908.

———. *Strategic Points in the World's Conquest*. New York, Fleming H. Revell, 1897.

Murphey, Rhoads. "The City as a Center of Change: Western Europe and China," *Annals of the Association of American Geographers*, 44.4:349-362 (December 1954).

———. *Shanghai: Key to Modern China*. Cambridge, Mass., Harvard University Press, 1953.

North China Herald, Shanghai, 1896-1897, 1921.

Ober, C. K. *Luther D. Wishard*. New York, Association Press, 1927.

———. Collection, Y.M.C.A. Historical Library, New York.

Paterno, Roberto. "Devello Z. Sheffield and the Founding of the North China College," *Papers on China*, 14:110-160 (1960). Harvard University, East Asian Research Center.

Pence, Owen E. *The Y.M.C.A. and Social Need*. New York, Association Press, 1939.

Peter, William Wesley. Papers, Y.M.C.A. Historical Library, New York.

Peter, Mrs. William Wesley. Private manuscript, Scientists' Cliffs, Maryland.

"P'ing-min chiao-yü" 平民教育 (Popular education), *Hsin Chiao-yü* 新教育 (The new education); Chung-hua chiao-yü kai-chin she 中華教育改進社 (Chinese educational advancement society), vol. 4. Shanghai, October 1923.

Princeton Alumni Weekly. Princeton, N.J., 1900-1914.

Rawlinson, Frank. "The Y.M.C.A. in China," *Chinese Recorder*, 51.5:342-348, esp. p. 344 (May 1920).

Records of the General Conference of the Protestant Missionaries of China, May 10-24, 1877. Shanghai, American Presbyterian Press, 1878.

Records of the General Conference of the Protestant Missionaries of China, May 7-20, 1890. Shanghai, American Presbyterian Press, 1890.

Reid, Gilbert. *The Duty of Christian Missions to the Upper Classes of China.* Shanghai, American Presbyterian Press, 1888.

————. *Endorsements of the International Institute.* New York, Fleming H. Revell, n.d. but issued before April 1898.

————. *Glances at China.* London, The Religious Tract Society, 1892.

————. *Report of the Mission among the Higher Classes in China.* Warsaw, N.Y., apparently privately printed and distributed, 1897.

Religion and Social Service. *Literary Digest.* New York, Funk and Wagnall, March 17, 1917.

Reports of Foreign Secretaries (China), 1895-1926. Y.M.C.A. Historical Library, New York.

Ricci, Matthew. *China in the Sixteenth Century: The Journals of Matthew Ricci, 1583-1610.* Tr. Louis J. Gallagher. New York, Random House, 1953.

Richard, Louis. *Comprehensive Geography of the Chinese Empire.* Shanghai, T'usewei Press, 1908.

Richard, Timothy. *Conversion by the Million.* 2 vols. Shanghai, Christian Literature Society, 1907.

————. *Forty-Five Years in China.* London, T. Fisher Unwin Ltd., 1916.

Robinson, Arthur. Collection, Y.M.C.A. Historical Library, New York.

Ross, Edward Alsworth. *The Changing Chinese.* New York, 1911.

Rouse, Ruth. *The World's Student Christian Federation.* London, SCM Press, 1948.

Routzahn, E. C. *The Health Show Comes to Town.* New York, Russell Sage Foundation, 1920.

Schwartz, Benjamin. *In Search of Wealth and Power: Yen Fu and the West.* Cambridge, Mass., Harvard University Press, 1964.

Sec, Fong F. "Government and Missionary Education in China," *Chinese Recorder*, 56.3:158-164 (March 1915).

Soothill, W. E. *Timothy Richard of China.* London, Seely, Service and Co. Ltd., 1924.

Tientsin Chi-tu-chiao ch'ing-nien hui ssu-shih chou-nien chi-nien ts'e 天津基督教青年會四十周年紀念冊 (Memento of the Tientsin Y.M.C.A. fortieth anniversary). Tientsin, 1935.

192

Tsu, Yu-Yue. *The Spirit of Chinese Philanthropy*. New York, Columbia University, 1912.

U.S. Department of State. *Papers Relating to the Foreign Relations of the United States* (1900-1908). Washington, D.C., U.S. Government Printing Office, 1902-1912.

Wang, C. T. "A Brief Survey of the Social Service Work in China," *China's Young Men*. Shanghai, 1915.

Whitewright, J. S. "Pioneer Museum Work in China," *The Museums Journal*, February 1909, pp. 266-274.

Wishard, Luther B. *The Students' Challenge to the Churches*. New York, Fleming H. Revell, 1900.

———. "World Tour Correspondence." Wishard Papers, Y.M.C.A. Historical Library, New York.

World Service Reports. Boxes X 951.09, Y.M.C.A. Historical Library, New York.

Wu Chih-kang. "The Influence of the Y.M.C.A. on the Development of Physical Education in China." Ph.D. diss., University of Michigan, 1957.

Wu Lien-teh 伍連德. *Wu Lien-teh tz'u ch'uan* 伍連德自傳 (A plague fighter: Autobiography of a modern Chinese physician). Nan-yang Hsueh-hui 南洋學會 (Nan-yang Study Association), 1960.

Wu Lien-teh. "Early Days of Western Medicine in China," *Journal of the North China Branch of the Royal Asiatic Society*, 62:1-131 (1931).

Yen, James Yang-ch'u 晏陽初. "P'ing-min chiao-yü hsin yün-tung" 平民教育新運動 (The new movement for popular education), *Hsin chiao-yü*, vol. 5, no. 4, pp. 1008-1026.

———. *The Mass Education Movement in China*. Shanghai, The Commercial Press, 1925.

———. Papers, Y.M.C.A. Historical Library, New York.

Y.M.C.A. "Conference on the World-Wide Expansion of the Young Men's Christian Association Held at the White House." Proceedings, October 20, 1910.

Y.M.C.A. of Boston. *Catalogue of Library*. Boston, Frank Wood, 1876.

Young Men's Era. New York, 1891.

Young Men's Work. Peking Y.M.C.A., vols. III, IV, V, VI (1912-1913).

Yü Jih-chang 余日章. *Chung-hua Chi-tu-chiao ch'ing-nien hui shih-lu* 中華基督教青年会實録 (History of the Chinese Y.M.C.A.) Hui-yüan ts'ung-shu 会員叢書 no. 1, Shanghai, 1927.

Yui, David. Papers, Y.M.C.A. Historical Library, New York.

NOTES

ABBREVIATIONS

ABCFM   American Board of Commissioners for Foreign Missions, "North China," 1880–1890, Vol. 4, A–B, bound letters and documents, Houghton Library, Harvard University, Cambridge, Mass.

CNHSL   *Chung-kuo Chi-tu chiao ch'ing-nien hui shih-lu* (History of the Chinese Y.M.C.A.)

FS   "Reports of Foreign Secretaries" (China), 1895–1926, Y.M.C.A. Historical Library, New York

SSCN   *T'ien-chin Chi-tu chiao ch'ing-nien hui ssu-shih chou-nien chi-nien ts'e* (Memento of the Fortieth Anniversary of the Tientsin Y.M.C.A.)

WSCN   *Chung-hua Chi-tu chiao ch'ing-nien hui wu-shih chou-nien chi-nien ts'e* (Memento of the Fiftieth Anniversary of the Chinese Y.M.C.A.)

Note: Box numbers refer to China correspondence, Y.M.C.A. Historical Library, New York.

CHAPTER 1. THE SEARCH FOR COMMUNICATION

1. *Records of the General Conference of the Protestant Missionaries of China, May 10–24, 1877* (Shanghai, 1878), p. 31; cited hereafter as *1877 Conf.*

2. Ibid., Introduction. The men who suggested the meeting were John Nevius, Alexander Williamson, and J. B. Hartwell.

3. The provinces were Shantung, Chihli, Kiangsu, Hupeh, Kiangsi, Fukien, Chekiang, and Kwangtung.

4. The missionary sense of urgency is brilliantly described in Pearl Buck's biography of her father, *Fighting Angel* (New York, 1957, 1964).

5. See Walter N. Lacy, *A Hundred Years of China Methodism* (New York, 1948), esp. pp. 140–141, which describe the early years of the Foochow Mission School, started in February 1848.

6. Daniel W. Fisher, *Calvin Wilson Mateer* (Philadelphia, 1911), p. 121. Mateer went to China in 1863 to Tengchow, a port in Shantung fifty-five miles from Chefoo.

7. The three were Chauncey Goodrich, Chester Holcombe, and Arthur Smith. See *The Chinese Recorder and Missionary Journal* (Shanghai), 1877, p. 212.

8. See, for example, Marilyn Blatt, "Problems of a China Missionary," in *Papers on China*, 12:28–46 (1958, Harvard University, East Asian

194

Research Center). Justus Doolittle buried two wives and two children.
9. *Chinese Recorder,* 1877, p. 304.
10. Blatt, p. 32.
11. Lacy, p. 52.
12. For statistics, see *1877 Conf.,* pp. 481–488.
13. Many missionaries at the 1877 conference complained about the relative poverty of their congregations. For one of the clearest reports, see Y.M.C.A. publication in America, *Young Men's Era* (New York), Feb. 12, 1891, p. 99: "there are three grades in [Chinese] society— official, merchant, poor. Young men of the third class are practically the only ones as yet reached by the gospel."
14. See Paul A. Cohen, *China and Christianity* (Cambridge, Mass., 1963), for an examination of gentry and official opposition to Christianity.
15. Lacy, pp. 298–300.
16. At the 1877 conference, however, E. J. Dukes claimed that his congregation in Amoy had a few well-to-do men who supported his church. Presumably they were merchants. *1877 Conf.,* p. 297.
17. Pearl Buck's father was in more or less chronic disrepute with some of his colleagues over the peculations he tolerated in his converts. See Buck, *Fighting Angel* (1964), p. 159.
18. *1877 Conf.,* p. 294. The church was the American Presbyterian; the missionary, C. R. Mills.
19. The Methodist Episcopal Church ordained three Chinese as deacons and four as elders in 1869. By 1899 the second session of a newly organized central conference provided that half the ministerial delegates must always be foreign missionaries, but not until 1930 did the church elect Chinese bishops. Lacy, pp. 81, 91, 108.
20. *1877 Conf.,* p. 326.
21. Buck, *Fighting Angel,* passim; Blatt, p. 31.
22. *1877 Conf.,* p. 19.
23. Ibid., pp. 1–4, 60, 439, 442; Buck, *Fighting Angel,* p. 72.
24. *Chinese Recorder,* 1877, p. 246.
25. *1877 Conf.,* p. 177.
26. Cohen, p. 270.
27. Timothy Richard, *Forty-Five Years in China* (London, 1916), p. 140.
28. An attack by R. Nelson in *Chinese Recorder,* 1877, pp. 351–359. As the outraged Nelson pointed out, Mencius argued that human nature was good, whereas everyone knew it was evil, so how could Shang-ti be God?
29. *Records of the General Conference of the Protestant Missionaries of China, May 7–20, 1890* (Shanghai), p. 653; cited hereafter as *1890 Conf.* The speech appears on pp. 619–631.
30. Fisher, p. 110.
31. Miss Buck tells this story in several versions, in *My Several*

Worlds (New York, 1954), p. 199, and in *Fighting Angel,* p. 144, which involves a bandit instead of an old woman.

32. Cohen.

33. *1877 Conf.,* p. 105. J. Hudson Taylor claimed to know the man.

34. Ibid., pp. 234–235.

35. T. Richard, *Forty-Five Years in China,* p. 34.

36. There was much discussion about the Jesuits at the 1877 conference. See *1877 Conf.,* pp. 219 (Joseph Edkins's remarks), 230–231 (Martin's remarks).

37. Matthew Ricci, *China in the Sixteenth Century: The Journals of Matthew Ricci, 1583–1610,* trans. Louis J. Gallagher (New York, 1953), pp. 166–169, 275, 277, 279.

38. *1877 Conf.,* p. 200; Roberto Paterno, "Devello Z. Sheffield and the Founding of the North China College," in *Papers on China,* 14:119 (1960); *1877 Conf.,* pp. 49, 239.

39. *Chinese Recorder,* 1877, pp. 246–248.

40. Timothy Richard, *Conversion by the Million* (Shanghai 1907), I, 99.

41. T. Richard, *Forty-Five Years in China,* p. 53.

42. W. E. Soothill, *Timothy Richard of China* (London, 1924), p. 49.

43. T. Richard, *Forty-Five Years in China,* pp. 54, 156–158.

44. Ricci, pp. 275, 279.

45. T. Richard, *Forty-Five Years in China,* p. 80.

46. Ibid., pp. 54, 156–158.

47. Ibid., pp. 119–120.

48. T. Richard, *Conversion by the Million,* pp. 101–102.

49. T. Richard, *Forty-Five Years in China,* p. 149.

50. Gilbert Reid, *Glances at China* (London, 1892), pp. 123–124, 175–179; Gilbert Reid, *The Duty of Christian Missions to the Upper Classes of China* (Shanghai, 1888), a paper read before the Presbyterian missionaries of Shantung on Nov. 9, 1887, and before the Missionary Association of Peking on Jan. 27, 1888.

CHAPTER 2. YOUTH AND THE Y.M.C.A.

1. Paterno, p. 120.

2. S. C. Leung, "Sino-American Cooperation in Y.M.C.A. Work," mimeographed (Y.M.C.A., New York, November 1963), p. 2.

3. WSCN, pp. 170–173.

4. Paterno, pp. 139–140.

5. Harlan Beach to Judson Smith, Tungchow, July 20, 1885, ABCFM, item 230.

6. Beach to Smith, Tungchow, Oct. 30, 1886, ABCFM, item 232.

7. Beach to Smith, Tungchow, June 6, 1888, ABCFM, item 237.

8. C. Howard Hopkins, *History of the Y.M.C.A. in North America* (New York, 1951), esp. pp. 3–6. This chapter draws heavily on Professor Hopkins' book.

196

9. Hopkins, p. 107.

10. One example was the Young Men's Society of David Nasmith, formed in 1830–1831. After the Y.M.C.A. had been founded, many other groups were started, such as the Salvation Army in 1865, designed primarily to serve the classes neglected by middle-class service organizations, and the Young People's Methodist Alliance in 1883.

11. For an excellent discussion of the urbanization of America and its social problems, see Carl N. Degler, *Out of Our Past* (New York, 1962), ch. XI, esp. pp. 305–307, 314–320.

12. Y.M.C.A. of Boston, *Catalogue of the Library* (Boston, 1876).

13. Hopkins, esp. pp. 29, 89.

14. Ibid., pp. 81–84, 23. See also Frank Grenville Beardsley, *A History of American Revivals* (New York, 1912), ch. XII.

15. C. K. Ober, *Exploring a Continent: Personal and Associational Reminiscences* (New York, 1929), p. 44, quoted in Hopkins, p. 283.

16. There are many books on Moody. The information here is pieced together primarily from Hopkins and from J. Wilbur Chapman, *The Life and Works of Dwight L. Moody* (Philadelphia, 1900).

17. Beardsley, esp. pp. 118–186.

18. Chapman, p. 318; John Wesley Hanson, *The Wonderful Life and Works of Dwight L. Moody* (Atlanta, Georgia, n.d.), p. 148.

19. Ibid., p. 148.

20. Chapman, esp. ch. 7.

21. The story of Luther Wishard is pieced together from several sources: Hopkins, ch. 7, esp. pp. 276–282; Luther D. Wishard, "Address at 100th Anniversary of Haystack Prayer Meeting" (Williams College, Williamstown, Mass., Oct. 9–12, 1906, Box X970.4); David B. Lowry, "Luther D. Wishard," A. B. thesis, Princeton, 1951; Luther D. Wishard, *The Students' Challenge to the Churches* (New York, 1900).

22. Wishard, "Address at 100th Anniversary."

23. Hopkins, p. 288.

24. Ibid., p. 316. The secretary was Robert Orr.

25. C. K. Ober, *Luther D. Wishard* (New York, 1927), p. 106.

26. Harlan Beach to Judson Smith, Tungchow, Aug. 4, 1887, ABCFM, item 234.

27. Beach to Smith, Tungchow, Jan. 16, 1889, ABCFM, item 239.

28. Hopkins, p. 297.

29. Luther D. Wishard, "Student Christian Movement in Mission Lands," typescript identified as appearing in *The Missionary Record of the United Presbyterian Church*, December 1895, no. 2, pp. 339–342 (X970.4).

30. Beach to Smith, Tientsin, June 5, 1889, ABCFM, item 242.

31. *The Intercollegian*, 13.1:5 (October 1890).

32. *1890 Conf.*, pp. 735, 732, 571–572 (Joseph Edkins), 433, 619–659, 175.

33. Ibid., pp. xxxv, lix, 431, 453, 11–22, 169.

34. Ibid., pp. 141–145.

35. *The Intercollegian*, 13.3:49 (December 1890). See also L. D. Wishard, "Secretarial Letters," July 19, 1890, in C. K. Ober Collection, Y.M.C.A. Historical Library, N.Y.

36. Luther D. Wishard to "Fellow Students," May 15, 1890, in Ober Collection.

37. For example, in a general letter sent to possible donors, Wishard referred to the "very serious financial situation" in the foreign work. The draft, in the Wishard World Tour Correspondence, Wishard Papers, Y.M.C.A. Historical Library, is dated Oct. 24, 1892.

CHAPTER 3. THE BEGINNINGS OF SINO-WESTERN COOPERATION

1. *North China Herald*, May 15, 1896, p. 758. The essay topic, wrote the paper's "Shansi correspondent," caused an "immense stir."

2. *North China Herald*, Jan. 17, 1896, p. 85.

3. J. S. Whitewright, "Pioneer Museum Work in China," *The Museums Journal*, February 1909, pp. 266–274.

4. For a discussion of traditional Chinese cities, see Wolfram Eberhard, "Data on the Structure of the Chinese City in the Pre-Industrial Period," *Economic Development and Cultural Change*, 4.3:253–268 (April 1956); Rhoads Murphey, "The City as a Center of Change: Western Europe and China," *Annals of the Association of American Geographers*, 44.4:349–362 (December 1954).

5. Quoted in Chen Chi-yun, "Liang Ch'i-ch'ao's 'Missionary Education': A Case Study of Missionary Influence on the Reformers," *Papers on China*, 16:101 (1962).

6. China, Imperial Maritime Customs, *Decennial Reports on Trade*, Second Issue, 1892–1901, Statistical Series no. 6, I, 506 (Shanghai, 1904), citing Ernest Box in *North China Herald*, Oct. 17, 1898.

7. Mrs. Arnold Foster, *Chinese Schoolgirls* (London, 1909), p. 72.

8. *National Geographic*, 2.7:293 (July 1900); Louis Richard, *Comprehensive Geography of the Chinese Empire* (Shanghai, 1908), p. 76.

9. Archibald Colquhoun, *Overland to China* (New York, 1900), pp. 168–169.

10. Ibid., p. 167.

11. Gilbert Reid, *Glances at China*, p. 141.

12. Gilbert Reid, *Report of the Mission Among the Higher Classes in China* (Warsaw, N.Y., 1897), a pamphlet apparently privately printed and distributed. The officials are hard to identify because their names are not given, but one was probably Chang Yin-huan, who was minister to the United States in 1885 and who negotiated the restriction of immigration by Chinese laborers. He returned to Peking in 1890, became a member of the Tsungli Yamen, and in 1892 was named senior vice-president of the Board of Revenue, where he became an intimate of Weng T'ung-ho. Chang's friendship was evidently valuable to Reid.

13. Ibid.

14. Ibid., and Reid, *Endorsements of the International Institute* (New York, n.d.).

15. Peking missionaries to International Committee of the Y.M.C.A., 1891 (Box 67, I).

16. Willard Lyon to Richard C. Morse, Nov. 8, 1895, in D. W. Lyon Papers, Y.M.C.A. Historical Library.

17. Shanghai missionaries to International Committee, Feb. 1, 1891 (Box 67, I).

18. Chefoo missionaries to International Committee, June 17, 1893 (Box 22, C).

19. The most important sources for this composite picture of Tientsin are Louis Richard; British Naval Staff, Intelligence Division, *Handbook of China, vol. I General* (1918), 131–132. The trade statistics are from Cheng Yu-kwei, *Foreign Trade and Industrial Development of China* (Washington, D.C., 1956), p. 23.

20. George Candlin and H. J. Bostwick to Lyon, Oct. 25, 1895 (Box 67, I).

21. Knight Biggerstaff, *The Earliest Modern Government Schools in China* (Ithaca, 1961), pp. 47–80, esp. 67, 68.

22. Lyon to William Murray, Feb. 4, 1897 (Box 22, C).

23. Emily F. Bostwick to her cousin Kenneth, April 2, 1917, Y.M.C.A. Historical Library (Box 22, C).

24. D. W. Lyon, "The Present Situation in China," in *Foreign Mail*, June 1897, found in a notebook called "History of the Tientsin Y.M.C.A. and Related Papers, 1897" (D. W. Lyon Papers, Y.M.C.A. Historical Library); Lyon to Murray, Feb. 4, 1897 (Box 22, C).

25. Emily F. Bostwick to her cousin Kenneth, April 2, 1917 (Box 22, C).

26. David Yui, CNHSL. See also Kenneth Latourette, *World Service* (New York, 1957), esp. pp. 48, 50, 65.

27. For example, in May Lyon was reported to be trying to get $100 apiece from one hundred men in the United States. John W. Decker to Richard Morse, May 31, 1896 (Box 67, H).

28. Hopkins, p. 357.

29. *North China Herald*, June 25, 1897, p. 1136.

30. Hopkins, ch. 9, esp. p. 367.

31. Fletcher Brockman, FS 1909.

32. Willard Lyon report, Jan. 20, 1896 (Box 67, I).

33. The untitled pamphlet is undated but probably is an 1896 issue. It is kept in Box 67 of that date at the Y.M.C.A. Historical Library and refers specifically to English-speaking young men.

34. Yui, CNHSL.

35. *North China Herald*, April 2, 1897, p. 587.

36. Willard Lyon, "First Quarter Report," 1897 (Box 67, I).

37. "Meetings of Board of Directors, Tientsin," Dec. 7, 1897, in "History of the Tientsin Y.M.C.A. and Related Papers, 1897."

38. "Meetings of Board of Directors, Tientsin," July 10, 1896, in "History of the Tientsin in Y.M.C.A. and Related Papers, 1897"; pp. 112–113.

39. Knight Biggerstaff, "Shanghai Polytechnic Institution and Reading Room: An Attempt to Introduce Western Science and Technology to the Chinese," *Pacific Historical Review* (May 1956), pp. 127–149.

40. Robert Gailey, "Report for Six Months Ending Dec. 31, 1898" (Box 67, H).

41. Lyon announced his decision to put out a bulletin corresponding to one called "Young Men of India" in a letter to Richard Morse, May 28, 1896 (Box 22, C).

42. Lyon to Murray, Feb. 4, 1897 (Box 22, C).

43. Gailey, "Six Months Report."

44. Yui, CNHSL, p. 9.

45. Lyon to Morse, Dec. 16, 1895 (Box 22, C).

46. Lyon, "First Quarter Report," 1896; "Report Letter," Jan. 20, 1896 (Box 67, I). The students raised 100 taels for the land.

47. Yui, CNHSL, p. 2, laid great emphasis on the indigenization of the Association, but he was writing during the nationalistic upsurge of the 1920's and making his point to neutralize the growing feeling that the Y.M.C.A. had foreign connections and should not be supported. At the time Yui was national secretary of the Chinese Association.

48. The four that were probably functioning in 1896, excluding Tientsin, were Chefoo (founded 1893), Tungchow (1886), Foochow (1885), and probably Hangchow (1886) at the Presbyterian High School.

49. Lyon, "Quarterly Report," second quarter, 1896, which lists twenty mission school student Associations (Box 67, I).

50. D. W. Lyon, *The First Quarter Century of the Young Men's Christian Association in China* (Shanghai, 1920), p. 3.

51. Lyon to Morse, Nov. 24, 1896 (Box 22, C).

52. At the second convention in 1899, 102 delegates appeared from 24 colleges, and half were Chinese. In 1901 at the third convention, there were 131 Chinese and 25 foreigners.

53. John R. Mott, *Strategic Points in the World's Conquest* (New York, 1897), p. 141.

54. Robert R. Gailey, "The Chinese Y.M.C.A.'s in 1899, The Second National Convention," *The Chinese Intercollegian* (English Supplement, June 1899), p. 509.

55. "Third Annual Meeting of Tientsin Y.M.C.A." (Box 67, E), shows as elected in 1899: M. L. Taft, president; Tong Fu-min, vice-president; Wang Chung-yu (Tientsin University), recording secretary; Chung Wen-ao (Tientsin University), collector; Wang Kok-shan (Chinese Engineering and Mining Company), treasurer.

56. Lyon to John Mott, March 9, 1899 (Box 22, C).

57. Robert Lewis to Mott, Feb. 1, 1900 (Box 66, E).

58. Lyon to Mott, April 30, 1900 (Box 66, E).

200

59. Reid, *Endorsements.*

60. *North China Herald,* May 14, 1897, pp. 863–864, reporting a speech of April 30 before the North China Tract Society.

61. The Association voiced this opinion openly later. On Oct. 26, 1903, C. H. Robertson wrote that Reid's appeal to the Chinese was great and that his plan was the "Association" with the "Christian" left out (Box 66, A).

62. Lyon, "First Quarter Report," 1897 (Box 67, I).

63. Lyon to Morse, May 5, 1896 (Box 22, C).

64. Mott, *Strategic Points,* pp. 154–155, 160.

65. Robert Gailey, "January 1899 Report" (Box 67, E).

66. In an unpublished, unpaged manuscript by Robert Lewis (X970.4) at the Y.M.C.A. Historical Library, there is a record of a luncheon party at the Astor House in Shanghai presided over by Dr. W. W. Yen, graduate of the University of Virginia. Guests were Count Portalis of Paris, president of the Paris Y.M.C.A., and Samuel Woodward of Washington, department store owner and president of the Washington Y.M.C.A. Lewis sat at the table with "Chu Bau San" (Chu Pao-san, president of the Chinese Chamber of Commerce.) The luncheon was probably held in 1900.

67. Lyon to Mott, Feb. 1, 1900 (Box 66, E).

68. Gailey, "The Chinese Y.M.C.A.'s in 1899."

CHAPTER 4. ALLIANCE AND CHANGE, 1900–1911

1. John W. Foster, "Present Conditions in China," *National Geographic,* 17.12:651–672, 709–711, esp. pp. 668–672 (December 1906).

2. Li Chien-nung, *The Political History of China, 1840–1928,* tr. Ssu-yu Teng and Jeremy Ingalls (Princeton, 1956), p. 191.

3. Eugene Barnett, "General Report," Jan. 20, 1911 (Box 62, B). In the demonstration he saw, led by Wu T'ing-fang, there were about two thousand in the audience, mostly young men "of the better class."

4. Max Exner, FS 1910.

5. Fletcher Brockman, "The Outreach of the Y.M.C.A.," unpub. ms. of a speech, n.d., probably around World War I, Brockman Papers.

6. C. H. Robertson, "letter number 16," Oct. 8, 1906 (Box 23, A).

7. Brockman note "for a very limited circulation," Dec. 4, 1905 (Box 65, D).

8. A Chinese official to Lyon, noted in Lyon, FS 1908.

9. Gilbert Reid, *Report of the Mission.*

10. John Grant Birch, *Travels in North and Central China* (London, 1902), esp. pp. 227–232. Birch met Chu Ling-kwang—a taotai, director of the Szechwan Board of Mines, and brother of a Yung Wing boy (Chu Pao-fay?)—and Li Shin-ti, educated at the Foochow Arsenal and in France, who was described as "head of Viceroy Kuei's Foreign Office." Birch was most impressed by their eagerness for reform.

11. Reid, *Endorsements of the International Institute of China* (New York, n.d. but probably late 1897), pp. 4–5. For leadership outside the cities, see Y. K. Leong and L. K. Tao, *Village and Town Life in China* (London, 1915).

12. Brockman, Aug. 22, 1902 (Box 22, E). Early in his career in China, when still permeated by a rather harsh theological influence, Brockman called the upper classes "a stronghold of Satan." FS 1901. He later abandoned this judgment.

13. See proceedings of Harvard University, "Conference on the Chinese Revolution of 1911," mimeographed (Portsmouth, N.H., Aug. 22–27, 1965), esp. Marie-Claire Bergere, "The Role of the Chinese Bourgeoisie in the Revolution of 1911"; Charles Hedtke, "The Genesis of Revolution in Szechwan"; Akira Iriye, "Public Opinion in Late Ch'ing China."

14. For example, William Lockwood hoped that he might adapt the best of the Western experience to China, not copy it. William Lockwood to "friends," March 10, 1905 (Box 65, E). Gailey often remarked on the need to be creative rather than imitative. For example, Gailey to Mott, July 30, 1904 (Box 65, F).

15. Lockwood to Mott, Jan. 30, 1906 (Box 23, A). See also Benjamin Schwartz, *In Search of Wealth and Power: Yen Fu and the West* (Cambridge, Mass., 1964), esp. p. 39, on the failure of Chinese society to educate the masses in terms of traditional moral values.

16. G. W. Leavitt, FS 1906.

17. Fletcher Brockman, *I Discover the Orient* (New York, 1935), p. 86.

18. Robert Lewis to Taotai Yuan, 1905 (Box 65, E).

19. William Lockwood, "Occasional Letters," "Welcome to Tuan-Fan [sic], 1908, W. W. Lockwood, Jr., Collection, Princeton, N.J.

20. Lyon to Mott, May 24, 1900 (Box 22, D).

21. For a general discussion of the connotation of *Ch'ing-nien*, see Marion J. Levy, Jr., *The Family Revolution in Modern China* (Cambridge, 1949), esp. pp. 84–89.

22. Charles Harvey, FS 1912.

23. Yen evidently knew Gailey quite early, but whether before 1900 is uncertain. According to L. N. Hayes (FS 1911), Yen's two sons were baptized, which indicated his close ties to the Western community.

24. Liang became minister of foreign affairs in 1908. Wu was minister to the United States.

25. For a biography of Tuan-fang, see Arthur W. Hummel, *Eminent Chinese of the Ch'ing Period, 1644–1912* (Washington, D.C., 1943–1944). Tuan-fang's influence threaded in and out of Association work during these years, not only as an official in good standing with the imperial government (he had accompanied the empress dowager to Sian), but also as a reform-minded Manchu. He was acting governor general of Liang-Kiang in 1904, and in 1905 was picked to go abroad to observe Western governments. In August 1906 he was made governor general of Liang-Kiang and superintendent of foreign trade for the Southern ports.

202

He evidently was cordial to the extent of making donations to the Association and instructing his assistants to represent him at festive Association Y.M.C.A. occasions. He himself made an appearance at the Shanghai Y.M.C.A. in 1908.

26. Robert Lewis, FS 1906.

27. Monlin, Chiang, *Tides from the West* (New Haven, 1947), pp. 47–52.

28. Li Chien-nung, p. 191.

29. William W. Lockwood, "Summary of Wu T'ing-fang's remarks on laying of cornerstone of Boys' Building, March 7, 1914," in "Occasional Letters," W. W. Lockwood Papers, Princeton, N.J.

30. The passport bureau was certainly in existence by 1910 and probably before.

31. For example, Frank Lenz, long a secretary in the Chinese Y.M.C.A., started out in Association work as an official greeter for Chinese students docking in San Francisco.

32. Brockman, Dec. 4, 1905 (Box 65, D), headed "for very limited circulation." One Shanghai Association member was secretary to Tsaitse of the Imperial Commission that went abroad to investigate Western government, and later members reportedly served several Szechwan officials.

33. *North China Herald*, May 18, 1906, p. 365.

34. Ernest Burton and Thomas C. Chamberlain, *Report of the Oriental Education Commission* (Chicago, 1909), p. 521.

35. Robert Lewis, untitled, unpaged ms., Y.M.C.A. Historical Library.

36. On April 21, 1909, Brockman sent a general report to Senator George Cox of Canada, with copies routed to Richard S. Colgate, Mrs. Cyrus H. McCormick, Sr., R. E. Olds, and John Wanamaker.

37. If Chinese businessmen had any doubts about the Association's connections, they were removed when Secretary of War William Howard Taft personally dedicated the new Association building in Shanghai in October 1907.

38. When Ernest Burton visited China, ostensibly under the auspices of the University of Chicago but subsidized by Rockefeller, Tuan-fang asked him, "What is your real purpose and what are Mr. Rockefeller's intentions?" Burton and Chamberlain, p. 522.

39. Clarence H. Robertson to Mott, Jan. 23, 1904 (Box 65, A).

40. Robert Lewis, general letter, August 1901 (Box 22, D).

41. Brockman, FS 1901.

42. Lockwood to "friends," March 10, 1905 (Box 65, E).

43. S. C. Leung, "Sino-American Cooperation in Y.M.C.A. Work," reported: "It affords youth opportunities for mingling with kindred spirits, for coming to meet new friends and for satisfying a fundamental desire for comradeship."

44. The recognition of the neglect of college work was a continuing theme. For example, Brockman (FS 1903) wrote that the "imperious demands" of the city Associations impeded college work.

45. Gailey, FS 1902 (Box 22, D).

46. Robert Lewis, general letter, August 1901 (Box 22, D).

47. Brockman to Mott, Jan. 2, 1903 (Box 66, A).

48. Brockman to Mott, Nov. 11, 1902 (Box 66, C); J. S. Whitewright, pp. 266–274.

49. J. S. Whitewright to Brockman, Jan. 13, 1903 (Box 65, F).

50. A. P. Parker to Mott, Nov. 17, 1902 (Box 66, C).

51. Brockman to Mott, April 27, 1903 (Box 66, A).

52. The biographical data on Robertson came from scattered sources, with the early information and the picture from *The 'Ol Debris,* the Senior Yearbook of Purdue University.

53. Brockman, FS 1903.

54. Brockman to Mott, Jan. 2, 1903 (Box 66, A).

55. Reid could not overcome the continuing suspicion of foreigners in Peking and finally established his International Institute in Shanghai, where it presented lectures, discussions on comparative religion and politics, etc. It seems to have been in full operation by about 1903.

56. Brockman, FS 1903.

57. Robertson to Mott, Jan. 23, 1904 (Box 65, F).

58. *Princeton Alumni Weekly,* 14.18:375–377 (Feb. 11, 1914). The data on Gailey came from several sources, including Brockman, FS 1903; interview with Mrs. W. W. Peter; Gailey letters and reports at Y.M.C.A. Historical Library.

59. There is a good account of this high school in SSCN, pp. 3–5 of English supplement.

60. Gailey, FS 1903.

61. L. N. Hayes, FS 1911.

62. Gailey, FS 1904, 1905.

63. Gailey, FS 1904.

64. Alice Gregg, *China and Educational Autonomy* (Syracuse, 1946), p. 27.

65. Gailey, FS 1903, 1905; Hayes, FS 1911.

66. Harvey, FS 1904.

67. U.S. Dept. of State, *Papers Relating to the Foreign Relations of the United States, 1905* (Washington, D.C., 1905), no. 97, p. 182.

68. Gailey, FS 1905.

69. Brockman to Lyon, May 1905 (Box 65, E).

70. Gailey, FS 1904; Robertson, FS 1906; Harvey, FS 1905.

71. Robertson, FS 1906.

72. Eugene Barnett to me, Dec. 8, 1962.

73. Brockman, FS 1906; Robertson, general letter, Jan. 31, 1906 (Box 65, C).

74. Gailey, FS 1906, 1908.

75. Wu Chih-kang, "The Influence of the Y.M.C.A. on the Development of Physical Education in China," Ph.D. diss., (U. of Michigan, 1957), p. 103.

204

76. This story has cropped up in a number of places, including William Lockwood to Dr. and Mrs. M. J. Exner, Aug. 28, 1908, "Occasional Letters."

77. Monlin Chiang, p. 24.

78. For information on the early period, see Wu Chih-kang; C. H. McCloy, *Physical Education in China* (Peking, 1923).

79. Wu Chih-kang, p. 97.

80. Gailey, FS 1904.

81. Wu Chih-kang, pp. 97, 103.

82. Robertson, FS 1908.

83. Brockman, FS 1903; Arthur Rugh, FS 1905.

84. D. Willard Lyon, *Chinese Students in Japan* (Shanghai, 1906), pp. 3–5.

85. Ibid., p. 7.

86. Ibid., p. 9.

87. Brockman to Mott, Sept. 17, 1906 (Box 23, A).

88. Burton St. John to friends, June 25, 1906 (Box 65, C); John Mott, *The Chinese Student Migration to Tokyo* (New York, 1908; copy in Box X619.252).

89. Brockman to Mott, Sept. 17, 1906 (Box 23, A).

90. Harvey, general letter, May 19, 1903 (Box 66, A), which compared the anti-Manchu feeling to the anti-British feeling of American colonists in 1776.

91. Lyon, FS 1907, remarked that it was well for China that she had many conservatives, and the church representatives in Tokyo serving at the Y.M.C.A. tended to echo this feeling.

92. C. T. Wang, Speech on Friday, Jan. 11, 1907 (Box 23, A). The box contains a notice of the formal opening of the Chinese Y.M.C.A. of Tokyo at Sanchome Mitoshirocho, Kanda.

93. Logan Roots, bishop of the Methodist Episcopal Church in China, wrote to Lyon on June 22, 1907 (Box 23, A), that he had heard from J. E. Williams of the Presbyterian Mission of Central China, a man assigned to Tokyo by his mission, that *Min Pao* was in the Y.M.C.A. rooms.

94. J. M. Clinton, FS 1908.

95. R. K. Veryard, Waseda Dept., Chinese Y.M.C.A., Tokyo, "Report for Quarter Ending Dec. 31, 1911" (Box X619.252), wrote that after the revolution, two Chinese secretaries (one of whom was Wang) resigned and went directly into the revolutionary party on the mainland. The majority of the Chinese, reported Veryard, proved to be enthusiastic revolutionaries, many having long been members of the society.

96. W. W. Lockwood, "Occasional Letters," contains a brief reference to a speech made by Lockwood in April 1912 to welcome Sun to the Shanghai Association. Lockwood introduced him as "not a stranger to the Young Men's Christian Association. He has for many years shown himself a friend to its work."

97. Logan Roots to Lyon, June 22, 1907 (Box 23, A).

98. Lyon to Roots, June 25, 1907 (Box 23, A).

99. Rev. Hardy Jowett, writing in the July 1908 edition of *The Chinese Student in Japan,* a conservative, English language pamphlet published by missionaries at least through 1908 (Box X619.252).

100. Brockman, FS 1912.

101. In Burton and Chamberlain, p. 690, Burton described Brockman: "In my judgment he is one of the most broad-minded, far-seeing and discreet men among those foreigners who are working for the settlement of China." On p. 722 he remarked of the secretaries: "The men have been chosen with better judgment on the whole than has been shown by any other missionary organization whose selections I have had occasion to observe carefully." On Oct. 20, 1910, at the invitation of President Taft, the Y.M.C.A. held a conference at the White House to raise money for world-wide expansion. Those interested in China who attended were John Mott, Fletcher Brockman, C. T. Wang, Logan Roots, and Burton. Their addresses and the other participants' are collected in a Y.M.C.A. booklet entitled "Conference on the World-Wide Expansion of the Young Men's Christian Association Held at the White House," Proceedings, Oct. 20, 1910. John Wanamaker offered to provide another building, his sixth, for the Orient, and John Rockefeller, Jr., in absentia, offered up to $540,000 if it could be matched. Half a million dollars eventually went to China for buildings.

102. D. Willard Lyon, *The First Quarter Century,* p. 6.

103. Lyon, "Quarterly Letter," Aug. 1, 1910 (Box 23, B).

104. "Stenographic Record of the Secretaries Conference" (Shanghai), May 7–14, 1912, p. 110 (Box 60, E).

105. Gailey, "First Years of Work for Young Men in Peking," Aug. 22, 1910 (Box 23, B).

106. Brockman, FS 1903.

107. The statistics and records prove virtually impossible to untangle if one wishes to make up lists. In one place D. W. Lyon referred to a Hankow Association by 1907; the White House Conference unequivocally stated that no Association existed there as late as 1910. Lyon reported ten cities "occupied" by 1907, but it is hard to understand just what he meant. Perhaps men had been sent to some of these cities to investigate the possibilities of starting work, as Robertson had been sent to Nanking in 1902 and subsequently left it. The important matter for this account is not the number of cities claimed, however, but the number where interesting and effective work was done.

108. By 1909 C. L. Boynton (FS 1909) wrote that the Chinese edition had sixteen pages of advertising, 5,214 paid subscriptions (of which 502 were in Japan), and a larger paid subscription list than any other Christian periodical in China. The journal contained a great deal of Association news and at this time was not an intellectual medium of news or opinion. Joining Zia on the editorial committee were P. S. Yie and Y. K. Woo.

206

109. General Report, 1909 (Box 23, B).

110. The Peking Association, especially Dwight Edwards, also shared in the Famine Relief fund.

111. Max Exner, FS 1910; *North China Herald,* Oct. 28, 1910, p. 221. Most of the audience were government school students.

112. Robert Service, Sept. 21, 1908, "Report of Y.M.C.A. Work in Chengtu, West China" (Box 23, A).

113. William Wilson to a Mr. Richardson, Oct. 8, 1912, from London (Box 60, C).

114. Service, FS 1910.

115. Robertson, FS 1908.

116. Robertson to Mott, Sept. 23, 1909 (Box 23, A).

117. Robertson, "The Neglected Upper Classes of China and Korea," Jan. 1910 (Box 23, B).

118. Robertson, FS 1910.

119. Robertson to Mott, Aug. 31, 1910 (Box 23, B).

120. Robertson, FS 1911.

121. Robertson, FS 1910.

122. Roscoe M. Hersey, *Social Service* (Shanghai, 1914, 3rd edition), Y.M.C.A. Historical Library.

123. Brockman to Sen. George Cox, April 21, 1909 (Box 23, A). Brockman nevertheless considered athletics still by far the best way to reach students.

124. Brockman, FS 1912.

125. For an appraisal of Chinese work, see Tsu Yu-Yue, *The Spirit of Chinese Philanthropy* (New York, 1912), esp. pp. 23–29.

126. John Stewart Burgess to a Prof. Miller, Dec. 26, 1910 (Box 62, D).

127. Brockman, "Annual Report Ending Sept. 30, 1911" (Box 61, C).

128. C. T. Wang to Mott, Jan. 13, 1912 (Box 23, B).

CHAPTER 5. THE Y.M.C.A. AND COMMUNITY ACTION

1. *North China Herald,* Oct. 29, 1921, p. 324.

2. John Stewart Burgess, "First Quarter Report, 1912," John Stewart Burgess Papers.

3. Schwartz, p. 49.

4. Edward Alsworth Ross, *The Changing Chinese* (New York, 1911), p. 83. For an excellent description of the economic distress of China, see pp. 70–111.

5. Anon., "The Present Educational Conditions in China," *Chinese Social and Political Science Review,* 5.3:298, 303 (September, 1920).

6. Tsu Yu-Yue, p. 91.

7. Schwartz, p. 70.

8. John Stewart Burgess, *The Guilds of Peking* (Studies in History, Economics and Public Law, no. 308; Columbia University, New York, 1928), p. 207.

9. Tsu Yu-Yue, pp. 29, 90.

10. Huang I-feng, "Kuan-yu chiu Chung-Kuo mai-pan chieh-chi ti yen-chiu," Li Shih Yen-chiu, no. 3 (1964), pp. 89–116.

11. Interview with Eugene Barnett.

12. Brockman, FS 1912.

13. Hugh Moran to Mott from Wuchang, "Second Quarter Report, Aug. 12, 1912" (Box 60, D); R. S. Hall to Mott, July 22, 1912 (Box 60, D).

14. T'ang Shao-yi and Wang Ch'ung-hui had been backers from the start. Li Yüan-hung was an admirer; and Wang Kok-sĥan, a member of the Yüan Shih-k'ai circle, had been an officer of the Tientsin Association.

15. "Stenographic Record of the Secretaries Conference" (Shanghai), May 7–14, 1922, pp. 125, 44, 45 (Box 60, E).

16. Ibid., p. 87.

17. An Hour-a-Day School was located in Shanghai in 1913. It taught English.

18. In regular publications the Association used easy wen-li or classical style, but in health work and other attempts at popular education it began to use pai-hua or vernacular style.

19. J. H. Crocker was lent to the Olympic Committee in 1914 to train athletes for the Shanghai games.

20. "Stenographic Record, 1912," pp. 108, 97.

21. Burgess, FS 1912, "Conference of Government School Students at Wo Fo-ssu, Oct. 5, 1912."

22. The six colleges were Peking University; Hui-wen, the Government College; Tao-hsüeh yüan, the Union Theological Seminary; Tsing Hua University; I-hsüeh t'ang, the Union Medical College; and Shui-wu hsüeh-t'ang, the Customs College. See Hui-wu chi-wen, known in English as Young Men's Work, 3:4 (Peking, October 1912), Burgess Papers. Page 4 of Chinese version.

23. Charles Harvey, FS 1912.

24. "Report," Burgess Papers, Nov. 10, 1912.

25. Ibid.; Burgess Papers, Dec. 30, 1912.

26. Burgess Papers, Jan. 29, 1913. The lecturers were Dr. E. O. Brown of Vanderbilt University, a Dr. Willett of the University of Chicago, and Dr. W. B. Weatherford, a traveling Y.M.C.A. secretary for the southern United States.

27. Burgess Papers, April 8, 1913.

28. "Peking Y.M.C.A. Student Work Report, 1914," Burgess Papers.

29. Scattered information from Burgess, FS 1913–1914, 1914–1915.

30. Hersey, p. 6.

31. Young Men's Work, October 1912.

32. Burgess, "Annual Report, 1914–1915" (World Service Reports, X951.09).

208

33. "Report of Work of the Peking Social Service Club," April 1914–1915, pamphlet, Burgess Papers.

34. Burgess, "Peking as a Field for Social Service" (Box 23, B).

35. Hersey, pp. 5–7.

36. Burgess, "Peking as a Field for Social Service."

37. Hersey, p. 36.

38. Ibid., p. 15.

39. Ibid., p. 23.

40. Ibid., pp. 9–10, 16–17.

41. Brockman, I Discover the Orient, pp. 134–135.

42. C. H. Robertson, FS 1912, "Through Science to Evangelism."

43. Wu Lien-te, Wu Lien-te Tz'u Ch'uan (Nanyang Hsüeh-hui—Nanyang Study Association, 1960); Wu Lien-te, "Early Days of Western Medicine in China," Journal of the North China Branch of the Royal Asiatic Society, 62:1–31 (1931).

44. C. L. Boynton, FS 1911.

45. From a biography of Dr. Peter handwritten by Mrs. Peter, which she kindly let me see in 1964. The manuscript quotes from a letter by Peter to Brockman, Feb. 20, 1912.

46. Hollis Wilbur memo, Sept. 30, 1912 (Box 60, C).

47. Report from W. W. Peter, n.d. but noted "received Aug. 25, 1913" (Box 61, D).

48. Brockman to Harry Pratt Judson, June 12, 1914 (Box 79, C).

49. G. H. Cole, FS 1914.

50. Robertson, FS 1915.

51. In February 1915, the Council on Public Health of the CMMA was formed, and in January 1916, a National Medical Association of Chinese foreign-trained doctors was founded.

52. E. C. Routzahn, The Health Show Comes to Town (New York, September 1920), pp. 3–30.

53. Peter Ms.

54. Anon., "Religion and Social Service," Literary Digest (March 17, 1917), pp. 708–709.

55. Routzahn; pictures from W. W. Peter Papers, Y.M.C.A. Historical Library.

56. Peter Papers.

57. "Religion and Social Service."

58. Hersey, FS 1915.

59. Cole, FS 1914.

60. Routzahn.

61. Ibid.

62. Burgess, "Annual Report, 1914–1915."

63. In 1914 Yüan Shih-k'ai got a Forest Law enacted. In 1916 a forestry service was started, but was discontinued at Yüan's death.

64. Fong F. Sec, "Government and Missionary Education in China,"

Chinese Recorder, 56.3:158–164 (March 1915); anon., "The Present Educational Conditions," *Chinese Social and Political Science Review,* 5: 275–308 (1920).

65. Eugene Barnett to Brockman, March 31, 1916; July 1, 1916 (Box 23, D).

66. L. Newton Hayes, FS 1917–1918.

67. O. R. Magill, "Report for Quarter Ending March 31, 1915" (World Service, X951.09).

68. Robertson, FS 1915.

69. Cole, FS 1916; David Yui newsletter, July 13, 1917 (World Service, X951.09).

70. Ibid.

71. Judith Blick, "The Chinese Labor Corps in World War I," *Papers on China,* 9:122–126 (1955); Ta Chen, "Chinese Migrations, With Special Reference to Labor Conditions" (U.S. Department of Labor, Washington, D.C., 1923), pp. 145–146 (list of labor corps locations), 152–153 (social and welfare organizations).

72. "The Chinese in France. A Call to Service" (Y.M.C.A. pamphlet, n.d.), in my possession.

73. Y. C. James Yen, "The Popular Education Movement," typed report, April 1924, p. 4 (Box 37, B). See also Eugene Barnett's record of conversations with Yen, Jan. 4, 1925, Yen Papers, Y.M.C.A. Historical Library.

74. Lawrence Hall, letter, n.d., Yen Papers.

75. Yen, "The Popular Education Movement," p. 4.

76. Mrs. W. W. Peter Ms., Scientists' Cliffs, Maryland. See also G. H. Cole, "Annual Report, 1920" (World Service, X951.09) where he claimed to have trained the men in France.

77. G. H. Cole to "Frank" (Frank Lenz), Dec. 27, 1925 (Box 71, B).

78. J. C. Clark, FS 1919; J. C. Clark to Lyon, May 13, 1920 (Box 76, B).

79. E. H. Munson, "How Foochow Fought Cholera," W. W. Peter Papers, Y.M.C.A. Historical Library.

80. Y. C. James Yen, *The Mass Education Movement in China* (Peking, 1925), pp. 3, 11; *Hsin chiao-yü,* "P'ing-min Chiao-yü," 4:383–388 (October 1923), and "P'ing-min chiao-yü hsin yun-tung," 5:1008–1026 (December 1922).

81. L. J. Hall, letter, n.d., Yen Papers.

82. David Yui to Edward Jenkins, Feb. 23, 1921 (Box 24, B). In 1920 industrial work began, with extension programs in Shanghai factories, a hut in Pootung (the working class section of the city), similar activity in Wuchang, and plans for Kaifeng. The Association wanted to stay neutral in the antagonism between capital and labor, but realized that it would be increasingly difficult not to identify with either side.

83. L. J. Hall, n.d., Yen Papers.

210

84. Yen, "The Popular Education Movement," pp. 6–10.

85. Yen, *The Mass Education Movement,* pp. 5, 6, Yen Papers.

86. Yen to J. C. Clark, July 14, 1922, Yen Papers.

87. Yen, *The Mass Education Movement,* pp. 11, 12.

88. C. H. Robertson, "Foundation Work for the Chinese Republic," September 1923 (2-page letter in my possession).

CHAPTER 6. STUDENTS AND REVOLUTION

1. Arthur Rugh, FS 1918–1919.

2. George Fitch and S. K. Tsao to E. C. Pearce, June 21, 1919 (Box 23, E).

3. Ibid.

4. Dwight Edwards, "The Fight for Personal Democracy in China," typescript lent by Mr. Edwards, n.d., D. W. Edwards Papers, Y.M.C.A. Historical Library.

5. H. A. Wilbur, "Answers to Questions for 1920 Sent to Secretaries" (Box 24, B).

6. David Yui to O. R. Magill, May 17, 1921 (Box 75, B).

7. H. A. Wilbur, "Answers to Questions for 1920."

8. John Childs, "Annual Report, 1921" (Report letter, August 7, 1921) (World Service, X951.09).

9. Owen E. Pence, *The Y.M.C.A. and Social Need* (Associated Press, N.Y., 1939), p. 200.

10. David Yui, "Report of the *China Press*," August 24, 1920 (Box 24, A).

11. Clarence Shedd, "Statement of Returned Laborer Work," May 26, 1920 (Box 24, A).

12. See Box 24 for considerable data on early Y.M.C.A. industrial work.

13. Lockwood to Edward Jenkins, April 3, 1921 (Box 24, B).

14. Box 76, D, n.d. but probably February 1920.

15. Frank Rawlinson, "The Y.M.C.A. in China," *Chinese Recorder,* 51.5:342–348, esp. p. 344 (May 1920).

16. Yui to Jenkins, Feb. 23, 1921 (Box 24, B).

17. Lockwood to C. A. Herschleb, "Memo on Industrial Work of Shanghai," March 8, 1922 (Box 24, C).

18. Wilbur to Lyon, Nov. 29, 1922 (Box 24, C).

19. Eugene Barnett, "Notes on Visit of Eugene E. Barnett to Hankow," Dec. 13–19, 1926, p. 22 (Box 95, A).

20. M. T. Tchou, "The Labour Problem in China and the Aims of the Industrial Work of the Y.M.C.A.," n.d. but probably 1923 (Box 73, D).

21. J. L. Childs to Jenkins and Herschleb, June 4, 1924 (Box 72, F); John Stewart Burgess, "The Training of Social Workers in China," an address given in Nanking, February 1924, (Box 72, E).

22. See, e.g., Box 73, and 1923 Annual Reports (Box 24).

23. T. C. McConnell, FS 1920.

24. Eugene Barnett, "Autobiography," typescript (Washington, D.C., 1962), Ch. XIII.

25. Chow Tse-tsung, *The May Fourth Movement* (Cambridge, Mass., 1960), p. 321.

26. "Conference with Christian Leaders of Nanking," Feb. 29, 1920 (Box 76, E).

27. J. L. Childs, "Annual Report," 1921 (World Service, X951.09).

28. W. J. Wen to "K. C." (last name unknown), Feb. 20, 1920 (Box 24, B, also Box 76).

29. Chow Tse-tsung, pp. 322, 324.

30. "Declaration of the Non-Christian Students Federation," March 19, 1922, Edwards Papers.

31. D. W. Edwards, "The Anti-Christian Movement in China," n.d., Edwards Papers.

32. For lengthy discussion, see Barnett, Ch. XIII.

33. "1923 Statistical report of City Young Men's Association of China, Year Ending Dec. 31," (Box 73, A).

34. *China National Reports,* statistics for 1922, Y.M.C.A. Historical Library.

35. Arthur Rugh to Mott, March 10, 1919 (Box 85, E).

36. "1923 Report" (Box 24, C); Sun's speech in WSCN, p. 1.

37. "Suggested Topics for Preliminary Consideration in Preparation for the Conference of General and Associate Secretaries of the Young Men's Christian Association of China, To Be Held in Hangchow, May 24–June 3, 1924" (Box 72, G).

38. "Suggested Topics for Preliminary Consideration in Preparation for the Conference of General and Associate Secretaries of the Young Men's Christian Association of China, To Be Held in Shanghai, July 27–August 9, 1925" (Box 71, E).

39. Yui to Mott, June 25, 1925 (Box 25, A).

40. "Notes on National General Secretaries' Conference," Shanghai, July 1925, p. 6 (in my possession).

41. T. K. Jones, "Report for 1925" (Box 24, D).

42. Yui, CNHSL.

43. "Student Situation in First Fifteen Cities," March 12, 1925 (Box 25, A).

44. See, e.g., long memorandum, J. W. Nipps to Brockman, Sept. 24, 1925 (Box 25, A).

45. "Translation of Certain Resolutions Regarding Anti-Christian Movement Adopted by the Seventh National Convention of the National Student Union of the Republic of China held in July, 1925," Edwards Papers.

46. Barnett, FS 1925.

47. Yui to Mott, June 27, 1925 (Box 25, A).

48. W. W. Brockman, "Annual Report," 1925 (Box 25, A).

212

49. R. K. Veryard, "Annual Report," 1925 (Box 71, A). .

50. S. M. Cowles, "Swatow, China, Christmas Day Anti-Christian Activities," Dec. 28, 1925 (Box 25, A).

51. Eugene Barnett, "Letter to Accompany Statistical Reports of the City Associations of China for 1925," July 1, 1926 (Box 95, C).

52. See "Notes on Visit of Eugene E. Barnett to Hankow," Dec. 13–19, 1926 (Box 95, A).

53. Ibid.

GLOSSARY

Ch'ing-nien hui 青年會
Chu-Fa Hua-kung chou-pao 駐法華工週報
Chu Pao-san 朱葆三
Chung-hua Chi-tu chiao ch'ing-nien hui 中華基督教青年會
Chung-kuo p'ing-min chiao-yü ts'u-chin hui 中國平民教育促進會
Chung Wei-i 仲偉儀
Chang Po-ling 張伯苓
chih, t'i, te, ch'ün 智, 體, 德, 羣
Chin-pu 進步
Fu, Daniel Jo-yü 傅若愚
Hsü Pao-ch'ien 徐寶謙
Hsüeh-hsiao pao 學校報
Lin, D. Y. (Ling Tao-yang) 凌道揚
Ma Pei-yüan 馬伯援
Ou-yang hsü-te 歐陽旭德
Pei-ching she-hui shih-chin hui 北京社會實進會
Sung, Paul Ju-hai 宋如海
Tchou, Thomas M. T. (Chu Mou-ch'eng) 朱懋澄
Ts'ao, S. K. (Ts'ao Hsüeh-keng) 曹雪賡
Wang Cheng-t'ing 王正廷
Wu Lien-teh 伍連德
Yen Hsiu 嚴修
Yen, James (Yen Yang-ch'u) 晏陽初
Yü Jih-chang 余日章
Yung, Frank Chien-ch'iu 雍劍秋
Zia, H. L. (Hsieh Hung-lai) 謝洪賚

INDEX

HARVARD EAST ASIAN SERIES